MENTORING HIS WAY

DISCIPLE TWELVE

VOLUME 1

Spiritual Characteristics
of a Godly Life

DR. ROY L COMSTOCK

Foreword by
Paul A. Cedar, D.Min./D.D.

ISBN 978-1-63575-289-2 (Paperback)
ISBN 978-1-63575-290-8 (Digital)

Christian Faith Publishing, Inc.
296 Chestnut Street
Meadville, PA 16335
www.christianfaithpublishing.com

Previously published by Christian Mentors Network

Printed in the United States of America

CONTENTS

Discussion questions are at the end of each chapter.

ACKNOWLEDGMENTS

There are many people that I could acknowledge as having helped me in my journey toward living a more Godly life. Though my ministry is primarily with men, it is a woman that has had the greatest impact on my spiritual walk. That woman is my wife, Sarah. She is teaching me how to love and how to give without expecting anything in return; she does it just for the love of it. Because of her example, I am learning how to love others more than I love myself. I pray that everyone will have the joy of knowing this relationship with their spouse that Sarah and I have. It is not always perfect, but we are both committed to glorifying God in all that we say and do. Thank you, Sarah. I love you with all my heart.

When I first started writing this book in prison, I asked myself this question, "What Biblical values have I compromised that caused me to be where I am and how do I explain to my children how to keep from making the same mistakes?" I want to acknowledge all of our children Denise and Roby, Mike and Ariana, and Michelle and Scott, and our beautiful grandchildren, for the great contribution they have all made to my life and ministry. It is a real joy to see how God has protected each of them and kept them in close relationship with Himself. I also want to acknowledge my oldest brother,

Alex, for standing by me through both the good and the bad times. Thank you all for your love and encouragement.

There are many others that I want to acknowledge without whom, this series of books would not have come to fruition. The graduates of my first training class were fellow inmates at the California Institution for Men. The superintendent and the chaplain gave me permission to lead a Bible study for the men who were permanently assigned to that prison. I wrote the lessons each evening and typed them during the day in the superintendent's office where I worked as a clerk. My friend and fellow inmate Billy Dugger, who I worked with in the office, retyped and edited the material so that it would be readable. At the end of the study, we graduated twenty-four inmates. Since then, many have completed this three-volume series resulting in transformed lives.

I sent the manuscript home to Sarah and she went over it and gave it to our friend Bob Root. Bob put it in the computer where he formatted it and prepared it for its first release and copyright in 1989. When I rewrote it as a mentoring practicum course for the International Bible Institute (IBI), my daughter-in-law, Ariana, edited the entire manuscript. Our daughter Michelle Nelson helped in the rewriting of this Godly Life series. She designed the book covers and developed a Mentors Guide for each of the three volumes.

Dr. Earle E. Williams, president and founder of IBI, as my personal mentor and friend for forty years, has encouraged and enabled me when I needed it most. I want to thank Dr. Paul A. Cedar, chairman of Mission America Coalition for writing the foreword and for being a faithful friend for over five decades. Dr. Jess Moody, former senior pastor First Baptist Church, Van Nuys, California, came to my office and confronted me and told me that I needed to get my life right with the Lord and he kept coming back until I made that decision. He recently sent me the following note: "God bless you, Roy. Yours is a great story. Every saint has a past and every sinner has a future. Keep reaching them for Jesus, my beautiful friend!"

I also want to thank the late Dr. W.P. "Tex" Rutledge, senior pastor of Praise Chapel of Santa Clarita, California, for being the senior mentor in our first mentor/discipler training classes. You will see his invaluable contribution throughout. Last, but not least, are my two friends, Bill Creitz and Patrick Campbell. Both, while participating in the mentor/discipler training classes, and on their own time, put hours into editing and rewriting this material with the hope that lives will be transformed into the "Image of Christ."

FOREWORD

Mentoring is in. It has become an immensely popular subject in our culture during the past few years. The challenge is that although some people are writing about it and many more are talking about it, there seems to be relatively few who are actually doing it. Jesus believed in mentoring. In fact, He spent the majority of His time during His three years of public ministry mentoring twelve men who He personally chose to be His disciples.

The Apostle Paul also believed in mentoring and he encouraged others to do the same. He instructed Timothy, one of the young men that he mentored, *"And the things you have heard me say in the presence of many witnesses entrust to reliable men who will also be qualified to teach others."* (II Timothy 2:2 NIV) To the believers in Thessalonica, Paul wrote, *"On the contrary, we worked night and day, laboring and toiling...in order to make ourselves a model for you to follow."* (II Thessalonians 3:8-9 NIV) Paul presented the ultimate model for mentoring when he wrote, *"Imitate me, just as I also imitate Christ."* (I Corinthians 11:1 NKJV)

Without a doubt, Jesus Christ is the one person who has ever lived who is fully-qualified to be a model for living for every one of us. Jesus alone is the ultimate model for our lives. Roy Comstock has come to understand that important truth. In his helpful three-volume series, Roy has identified twelve basic Biblical characteristics of a Godly life. He believes that one living a Godly life mentors automatically. These principles can be of great help to anybody who desires to follow Christ unreservedly and then to help others do the same.

This book has not been written by a perfect man or by one whose life has always been a model for others to follow. Roy's life has not always been easy. He, like all true Christians, has been and is a work of God in process. We may call this Roy Comstock's "Prison Epistle," since much of this material was written while he was serving a prison term. Roy became a Christian as a teenager after being raised in countless foster homes. He attended two Christian colleges and became successful in business. Roy has a great heart for evangelism, and has been used by God in many ways, including teaching Christian seminars.

At one point, major failure came into his marriage, his business, and his personal life. The good news is that, instead of departing from the faith, Roy repented and turned to Christ in a deeper way than ever before. He cried out to the Lord concerning his own life, and the Lord responded not only to his needs, but also taught him insights that can be of great help to anyone who desires to follow Jesus Christ. It was during his time in prison that the Lord revealed many of the principles that Roy Comstock calls the "twelve characteristics of a godly life."

The focus of this three-volume series is upon following Jesus Christ—the one who is the perfect model for all of our lives. He is available to be our mentor. The basic principles shared are both Biblical and practical. Volume one has to do with the spiritual characteristics, volume two is about personal characteristics, and volume three is concerned with lifestyle characteristics.

Together they help the reader to draw nearer to our Lord Jesus and follow Him more faithfully and effectively. As you begin the study of this book, I would encourage you to approach this material with prayer and openness to God. You do not need to agree with all of the teachings in order to be helped. Ask our Lord Jesus to teach you the principles of authentic Christian discipleship and mentoring. He is waiting to be your helper, teacher, and guide. I believe that He wants every one of us to exemplify His character.

Paul A. Cedar, D.Min./D.D.
Chairman
Mission America Coalition

INTRODUCTION

Be Conformed to the Image of His Son

This is the first book in a series about developing certain Godly characteristics that others will want to emulate. It is about being, not doing. We are to become mentors. A mentor is a person whose behavior others observe and then decide, consciously or unconsciously, to copy. Our desire is to develop Godly characteristics so that Christ's life will be reflected through us.

The challenge we give every person that goes through this mentor training is that you will, in turn, find twelve others in your lifetime that you will mentor. Remember that mentoring is more about who you are than about what you do. You can mentor your people as a group or one at a time. If you want to do something significant with your life, you should help twelve others become Christ-like in their lives. During Jesus' three-year ministry on earth, He gave His personal time to twelve men, who in turn, turned the world upside down. Have your people get their own books for personal use. Use your copy of this three-volume series that you have gone through and share your experiences with them. There is also a mentor's guide available for each volume. Please visit our website at www.christianmentorsnetwork.org.

What we do is a direct result of what we are. What we are is determined by our values. Our values determine our character, and our character determines our behavior. Ask yourself these questions: "Do the characteristics reflected in my life exemplify the world's values or those of Christ?" "When people spend time with me, do they go away desiring fame, wealth, material possessions, glamour, sexual pleasure or popularity, just to mention a few, or do they desire to be more like Christ?" and "What values do they desire as a result of observing my character?"

Volume one is about developing four spiritual characteristics. These characteristics are based on the premise that God has a purpose for each believer. That purpose is explained in the eighth chapter of Romans, verses 28 and 29. *"And we know that for those who love God all things work together for good, for those who are called according to his purpose. For those whom he foreknew he also predestined to be conformed to the image of his Son, in order that he might be the firstborn among many brothers."* God foreknew, in other words, He knew in advance, from the beginning of time, who would accept Christ as savior. Therefore, He had predestined or purposed what they should become. His purpose is that they should be conformed to the image of His Son. The word "conformed" means to be molded. The word "image" means likeness. In other words, God's purpose is that each believer be molded into the likeness of Christ. We are to become Christ-like. Our life is to exemplify the character of our Lord and savior Jesus Christ. When people observe us in everyday life, they should see Christ.

Only through studying God's Word, prayer, and the Holy Spirit's power can this be accomplished. We must come to an understanding of who we are in Christ. We must also experience the benefits of trusting and obeying Christ in everything. When this happens, we will have the joy and peace that the Bible promises. When we interact with other people, the loving character of Christ should be very apparent.

Being Godly is having a lifestyle that centers on being, not just doing or saying. Now, let's examine the spiritual characteristics of a Godly life. I pray that this book will mean as much to you as it has to me. My desire is to be so much like Christ that others can, *"Be imitators of me, as I am of Christ."* (I Corinthians 11:1)

Roy L. Comstock, Th.D.
Chairman and Founder
Christian Mentors Network, Inc.

Characteristic One

BEING A BELIEVER

I KNOW JESUS CHRIST AS MY
PERSONAL SAVIOR AND LORD

CHAPTER ONE

WHO DO YOU THINK I AM?

> "For God so loved the world, that he gave his only Son, that whoever believes in him should not perish but have eternal life." (John 3:16)

The first Spiritual Characteristic of a Godly life is having a personal relationship with Jesus Christ. For most of us, it's certainly true we know of someone famous. We may know all the statistics on our favorite baseball player. We may know all the movies our favorite stars made. We may have memorized every word of a song by our favorite musical artist. We may be quite familiar with our president and many of his ideas, characteristics, and beliefs. We may even believe in him and what he stands for. But do we know him personally? If we got into a jam or required his endorsement, would he support us? Chances are that unless you had a personal relationship with the president and spent a lot of time with him, you'd be hard pressed for a favor.

It's not enough to believe in God. The Bible says that even demons believe and tremble. You must know God personally through His Son Jesus. You cannot conform to the image of Christ unless you have Him at the center of your life. And you cannot exemplify Christ for others if you don't know Him. Knowing Christ means that you have assurance of eternal life because of your relationship with Jesus. In other words, you know you will be spending eternity in Heaven with Him.

I have a living, vibrant, personal relationship with Jesus Christ

I am sure that most of you already know Christ as your Lord and Savior. It is my desire that the following pages may help you to better understand how to share Him with others in a deeper way.

Some of you may not know that you can decide where you are going to spend eternity. Perhaps, you have tried many times to fill the spiritual emptiness in your life, but no matter what you do, it does not satisfy your needs. You have missed the mark in communicating with God. It could be you are involved in all the activities that you thought were necessary in order to please God, but you don't seem to be finding the answers.

Are you putting your faith in people and missing the opportunity to develop a personal relationship with God? Instead of finding God in a personal way, perhaps you merely saw the apparent hypocrisy of people in the church. Perhaps a judgmental, unforgiving, or unloving Christian has hurt you, or maybe it was a domineering pastor, or the harsh words of an insecure elder. This experience caused you to use the excuse that you didn't want anything to do with the church since all the members didn't practice what they preached or interpreted the rules to justify their own self-righteousness.

You were putting your faith in people, and missed the opportunity to develop a personal relationship with God.

You sense that there is a God and you know that you need Him, but you don't know how to find Him. Or you may have difficulty understanding the need for a personal relationship with Him. I want to take time here to explain why you should, and how you can develop a personal relationship with God through receiving His Son Jesus Christ.

Watching a live television broadcast, four renowned religious leaders were interviewed regarding their views on world events. It was profound how deeply each one portrayed his view of God—the catholic priest expressing a light and easy God; the protestant portraying the God of discipline and strength; the intellectual portraying himself as a god; and the muslim expounding the virtues of a god of peace and tolerance. Each one expressed God in his own image and through his own eyes. Needless to say, the mention of Jesus Christ stirred emotions.

Contrary to popular religious tolerance and the philosophies that embrace "all roads lead to God," Jesus Christ proves to be a troubling figure in history and to other religious beliefs. Jesus Himself proclaimed to the religious leaders of His day, "No man comes to the father, but by me." Blasphemer! Audacious! Well, how exclusive and unfair! What narrow-minded thinking! "So who is this Jesus Christ?," you might ask.

This is the most important question you will ever ask. For the answer to this question, we must look at what the Bible has to say. Let's start with Matthew chapter 16.

> *"Now when Jesus came into the district of Caesarea Philippi, he asked his disciples, "Who do people say that the Son of Man is?" And they said, "Some say John the Baptist,*

> *others say Elijah, and others Jeremiah or one of the prophets." He said to them, "But who do you say that I am?" Simon Peter replied, "You are the Christ, the Son of the living God." And Jesus answered him, "Blessed are you, Simon Bar-Jonah! For flesh and blood has not revealed this to you, but my Father who is in heaven."* (Matthew 16:13-17)

On the whole, our culture's depiction of Jesus is that He is a good teacher, a prophet, or He is compared to other religious leaders like Buddha or Mohammed. Some even compare Him to Gandhi. They often talk about the truths that Jesus taught that are included in most all religions. Isn't it amazing that so little is said about who Jesus claimed to be?

When Jesus asked His disciples, *"Who are people saying I am?,"* it seemed to be a rhetorical question. He didn't even respond to their answers. Because the important question is never what other people think about Jesus. The real question He wanted them and us to be able to clearly answer is: *"Who do you think I am?"*

JESUS CLAIMED TO BE THE MESSIAH

> *Jesus is, the Christ, the Messiah, the Son of the Living God*

Jesus' disciple, Peter, answered this question very directly. He said, *"You are the Christ, the Son of the living God."* That is when Jesus did respond because the answer to this question is of utmost importance. He not only responded to Peter's answer but He confirmed it by stating the following: *"Blessed are you, Simon Bar-Jonah! For flesh and blood has not revealed this to you, but my Father who is in heaven."* In this statement, Jesus claims to be the Messiah.

While talking to the Samaritan woman at the well, Jesus again makes this claim

> *"The woman said to him, "I know that Messiah is coming (he who is called Christ). When he comes, he will tell us all things." Jesus said to her, "I who speak to you am he." (John 4:25-26)*

Christ is revealed as Messiah to Mary by the angel Gabriel

> *"And behold, you will conceive in your womb and bear a son, and you shall call his name Jesus. He will be great and will be called the Son of the Most High. And the Lord God will give to him the throne of his father David, and he will reign over the house of Jacob forever, and of his kingdom there will be no end." And Mary said to the angel, "How will this be, since I am a virgin?" And the angel answered her, "The Holy Spirit will come upon you, and the power of the Most High will overshadow you; therefore, the child to be born will be called holy—the Son of God." (Luke 1:31-35)*

Jesus Christ has always been alive and is Himself God

We find in John chapter one that Christ is more than the Son of God. He is, in fact, God Himself. "*In the beginning was the Word, and the Word was with God, and the Word was God. He was in the beginning with God. All things were made through him, and without him was not anything made that was made.* (John 1:1-3)

These verses go so far as to tell us that Jesus Christ is God. The Living Bible says, *"Before anything else existed, there was Christ, with God. He has always been alive and is Himself God. He created everything there is—nothing exists that He didn't make."* The "Word" means Christ. In verse 14 it says, *"And the Word became flesh and dwelt among us, and we have seen his glory, glory as of the only Son from the Father, full of grace and truth."* Jesus in the flesh was God dwelling among us.

Jesus reveals Himself to Paul

The Apostle Paul had an experience that totally convinced him that Christ was who he claimed to be. Before that, Paul was determined that Christianity was evil and, until he met Christ on the road to Damascus, it was his duty to destroy the Christian movement altogether.

> *"But Saul, still breathing threats and murder against the disciples of the Lord, went to the high priest and asked him for letters to the synagogues at Damascus, so that if he found any belonging to the Way, men or women, he might bring them bound to Jerusalem."* (Acts 9:1-2)

The ninth chapter of Acts tells of the dramatic experience Paul had in coming to a personal knowledge of Jesus Christ. Verses 20-22 explain the powerful effect Paul's conversion had on the Jewish people of Damascus.

> *"For some days he was with the disciples at Damascus. And immediately he proclaimed*

> *Jesus in the synagogues, saying, "He is the Son of God." And all who heard him were amazed and said, "Is not this the man who made havoc in Jerusalem of those who called upon this name? And has he not come here for this purpose, to bring them bound before the chief priests?" But Saul increased all the more in strength, and confounded the Jews who lived in Damascus by proving that Jesus was the Christ." (Acts 9:20-22)*

As you may already know, Paul went on to be the writer of most of the epistles in the New Testament. I believe that one of his best explanations of who Christ is may be found in his writings to the Colossians.

> *"He is the image of the invisible God, the firstborn of all creation. For by him all things were created, in heaven and on earth, visible and invisible, whether thrones or dominions or rulers or authorities—all things were created through him and for him. And he is before all things, and in him all things hold together. And he is the head of the body, the church. He is the beginning, the firstborn from the dead, that in everything he might be preeminent. For in him all the fullness of God was pleased to dwell," (Colossians 1:15-19)*

Christ holds all things together with His Own Power

Jesus is who He claimed to be, or He was insane, or He was one of the biggest frauds the world has ever seen. And if

He is God, then we must all make a very important decision about what we are going to do with Christ. We must accept Christ for who He claims to be or reject Him completely as a lunatic. We can no longer just think of Him as a good teacher or a prophet or a religious leader. The conclusion we must draw from this is that Jesus is the Christ, the Messiah, the Son of God, and also God himself.

Jesus declares that He is the only way to heaven

Jesus says in John 14:6, "Jesus said to him, "I am the way, and the truth, and the life. No one comes to the Father except through me."

Jesus is saying here that the only way we can have a relationship with God the Father is through Him. In other words, Jesus is claiming that there is no other way to Heaven or eternal life except through Him. If He is who He claims to be, we must understand the consequences of not believing that Christ is the only way to Heaven.

I know that I have eternal life because I have Jesus Christ

"If we receive the testimony of men, the testimony of God is greater, for this is the testimony of God that he has borne concerning his Son. Whoever believes in the Son of God has the testimony in himself. Whoever does not believe God has made him a liar, because he has not believed in the testimony that God has borne concerning his Son. And this is the testimony that God gave us eternal life, and this life is in his Son. Whoever has the Son

> *has life; whoever does not have the Son of God does not have life. I write these things to you who believe in the name of the Son of God that you may know that you have eternal life." (I John 5:9-13).*

WHY DID JESUS CHRIST COME TO EARTH?

God created man in His own image so that He could have fellowship with us. In doing this, He gave man freedom of choice. We have the ability to either obey God or do our own thing. However, there are consequences for the choices we make.

The first man Adam chose to go astray. "*Therefore, just as sin came into the world through one man, and death through sin, and so death spread to all men because all have sinned.*" (Romans 5:12) *"All we like sheep have gone astray; we have turned every one to his own way; and the LORD hath laid on him the iniquity of us all."* (Isaiah 53:6) This, doing our own thing instead of God's will, is called sin. "*All have sinned and fall short of the glory of God.*" (Romans 3:23) Everyone fails to measure up to God's perfect standards. This failure is called sin. The Bible says, *"The wages of sin is death."* (Romans 6:23a) Wages are something we earn. Sin is the thing we have all done. The wage we have earned for our sin is death (eternal separation from God).

"If we say we have no sin, we deceive ourselves, and the truth is not in us."…If we say we have not sinned, we make him a liar, and his word is not in us. (I John 1:8, 10) God is perfect and holy. He cannot permit sin to enter His presence. Our sin separates us from God. Thus, through sin we face eternal death. We must realize that we are all in the same boat. We have all sinned. And our sin separates us from God.

God knew from the beginning of time that we would all sin. But because of His unconditional love for us, He gave us a way to overcome sin and death. *"For God so loved the world, that he gave his only Son, that whoever believes in him should not perish but have eternal life. For God did not send his Son into the world to condemn the world, but in order that the world might be saved through him."* (John 3:16-17) *For the wages of sin is death, but the free gift of God is eternal life in Christ Jesus our Lord."* (Romans 6:23)

God showed His great love for us by sending Jesus

Chapter One

WHO DO YOU THINK I AM?

Questions for home study and group discussion

Who did Jesus claim to be?
Matthew 16:13-17; John 1:1-4, 14; 14:6

How many people have sinned?
Romans 3:23

What are the wages of sin?
Romans 6:23a

What did God's unconditional love do for us?
John 3:16-17

How did God overcome sin's death penalty?
Romans 6:23b

Notes from My Mentor's Personal Testimony

Scripture Memory Chapter One

"For God so loved the world, that he gave his only Son, that whoever believes in him should not perish but have eternal life." (John 3:16)

CHAPTER TWO

ETERNAL LIFE IS A FREE GIFT

> *"And this is the testimony that God gave us eternal life, and this life is in his Son. Whoever has the Son has life; whoever does not have the Son of God does not have life. I write these things to you who believe in the name of the Son of God that you may know that you have eternal life."* (I John 5:11-13)

Eternal life is given to us as a free gift, but, like any gift, we must receive it to make it our own. *"But to all who did receive him, who believed in his name, he gave the right to become children of God,"* (John 1:12) God offers us this free gift, but we must receive it.

> *But what does it say? "The word is near you, in your mouth and in your heart" (that is, the word of faith that we proclaim); because, if you confess with your mouth that Jesus is Lord and believe in your heart that God raised him from the dead, you will be saved. For with the heart*

one believes and is justified, and with the mouth one confesses and is saved... For everyone who calls on the name of the Lord will be saved." (Romans 10:8-10, 13)

"the righteousness of God through faith in Jesus Christ for all who believe. For there is no distinction and are justified by his grace as a gift, through the redemption that is in Christ Jesus, whom God put forward as a propitiation by his blood, to be received by faith. This was to show God's righteousness, because in his divine forbearance he had passed over former sins." (Romans 3:22, 24-25a)

God accepts and acquits me and declares me not guilty

"But God shows his love for us in that while we were still sinners, Christ died for us. Since, therefore, we have now been justified by his blood, much more shall we be saved by him from the wrath of God. For if while we were enemies we were reconciled to God by the death of his Son, much more, now that we are reconciled, shall we be saved by his life. More than that, we also rejoice in God through our Lord Jesus Christ, through whom we have now received reconciliation." (Romans 5:8-11)

"For I delivered to you as of first importance what I also received: that Christ died for our sins in accordance with the Scriptures, that he was buried, that he was raised on

the third day in accordance with the Scriptures," (I Corinthians 15:3-4 TLB)

The gift of God is eternal life through Jesus Christ our Lord

If you believe that Jesus Christ is God's Son and that He died on the cross and shed His blood to cover your sins, that He was buried and rose from the grave on the third day to take victory over your sins, and that He has forgiven you of all your sins; then right now, you need to receive His free gift of eternal life. You can do this by sincerely repeating the following prayer:

> Dear Jesus, I receive you into my heart. I receive you as my personal Lord and Savior. I willingly repent of my sin and turn from my desire for the things of this world. My desire is to grow spiritually so that I can learn to conform to your image. Thank you for your free gift of eternal life. Thank you for forgiving me of all my sins, and enabling me to be born spiritually into your family. In Jesus' name, Amen.

A brutal tyrant who was sentenced to die a tortuous death in return for his life of subversion was contemplating his own demise when suddenly he is released and set free. By some absolutely astounding twist of fate, someone has taken his place. The criminal's destiny of death with absolutely no ray of light or hope had burst open into an astonishing reality—he has been set free! Somebody else had paid the ransom with His own innocent life's blood. The man on death row was Barabbas. The innocent man who took his place was Jesus.

There was nothing Barabbas could ever do to deserve his freedom or buy back his life. In the same way, Jesus Christ bought back our lives with His own blood. We deserve death. We can never earn our own freedom. "*For the wages of sin is death, but the free gift of God is eternal life in Christ Jesus our Lord.*" (Romans 6:23)

Jesus promises that when we open the door to our heart and ask Him to come in, He will come in. Jesus said, "*Behold, I stand at the door and knock. If anyone hears my voice and opens the door, I will come in to him and eat with him, and he with me.*" (Revelation 3:20) God does not lie. He must be faithful to His own Word. So we know that when we open the door to our heart and ask Jesus to enter, He must come in. You prayed, asking Jesus to come into your heart. So what did He do? Where is He right now? That's right! He is in your heart; and because of that, you know that you have eternal life.

> "*And this is the testimony that God gave us eternal life, and this life is in his Son. Whoever has the Son has life; whoever does not have the Son of God does not have life. I write these things to you who believe in the name of the Son of God that you may know that you have eternal life.*" (I John 5:11-13)

If you died right now, where would you go for eternity? That's right, heaven. Because the Bible says that if you have the Son, you have eternal life. And because you know that you have Christ in your life, you know that you have eternal life.

> *"Now to the one who works, his wages are not counted as a gift but as his due. And to the one who does not work but believes in him who justifies the ungodly, his faith is counted as righteousness," (Romans 4:4-5)*

> *"For by grace you have been saved through faith. And this is not your own doing; it is the gift of God, not a result of works, so that no one may boast." (Ephesians 2:8-9)*

If you could live a good enough life to meet God's holy standard, then Christ wasted His life here on earth by dying on the cross. Eternal life is a free gift, you receive it instantly the moment that you pray and invite Christ into your heart. In that moment, your eternal destiny changes from hell to heaven. The matter is settled for all eternity. Nothing can separate you from the love of Christ.

> *"What then shall we say to these things? If God is for us, who can be against us? He who did not spare his own Son but gave him up for us all, how will he not also with him graciously give us all things? Who shall bring any charge against God's elect? It is God who justifies. Who is to condemn? Christ Jesus is the one who died—more than that, who was raised—who is at the right hand of God, who indeed is interceding for us. Who shall separate us from the love of Christ? Shall tribulation, or distress, or persecution, or famine, or nakedness, or danger, or sword?"*

Nothing will ever separate me from the love of God

> *"...For I am sure that neither death nor life, nor angels nor rulers, nor things present nor things to come, nor powers, nor height nor depth, nor anything else in all creation, will be able to separate us from the love of God in Christ Jesus our Lord."* (Romans 8:31-35a, 38-39)

Most of you reading this book know Christ as your personal Savior, but some of you may realize that you have been living in the flesh, seeking pleasure more than the conformance to the image of Christ. God loves you and is ready to forgive you. He promises that if you will confess (acknowledge) your sin, He is faithful and just to forgive you and to cleanse you of all unrighteousness (I John 1:8-10). You can be restored to fellowship with your Heavenly Father by simply asking God to restore you. God wants to have fellowship with you. He waits like a loving parent ready to welcome you back. Pray the following prayer right now:

> Dear Father, I have sinned against you by going after my own fleshly desires. I am now willing to turn from the pleasures of this world. I desire instead to become like Christ. I want your perfect will for my life. Thank you for forgiving me and cleansing me from all unrighteousness. In Jesus' name, Amen.

SAVED BY FAITH NOT BY FEELINGS

You will respond to the experience of receiving Christ in the following manner:

I do not rely on my own feelings to know that I am saved

First, your mind or intellect agrees with the facts found in the Bible concerning your salvation. Second, your will accepts by faith those things you do not yet understand. Third, your emotions express the feelings of joy that accompany the peace that comes from knowing that you are now totally accepted by God.

You are completely justified in the sight of God. The word "justified" means that it is just as if you never sinned. A great burden has been lifted from you. This gives you a great feeling of relief. However, you cannot rely on these feelings to determine if you are saved or not. Your feelings change so you must put your faith in God's Word.

The feelings expressed by your emotions may change, but the facts in God's Word do not change. Your mind has accepted these facts. Put your faith in the facts. Don't put your faith in your feelings. Many people make the mistake of believing that they are only saved if they feel saved. Your salvation is never dependent on how you feel. It is only dependent on the fact that God's Word declares it and you accepted it by faith.

God's Word declares it and I have accepted it by faith

If you are reading this with questions about the reliability of the Scriptures and this is keeping you from making a decision to accept Christ as your Savior, I recommend that you read The Case for Christ, by Lee Strobel. This is a book written by a journalist who personally investigated the evidence for Jesus. He did this to prove that his wife's new faith in Christ could not be true. As a result of his two-year investigation, Lee accepted Christ as his Lord and Savior.

Lee's book was instrumental in helping a friend of mine, Ken Kline, to accept Jesus as his Lord and Savior.

THE KEN KLINE STORY

Ken was raised in a church that taught about Jesus and contributed to his general knowledge of Christ, but without emphasizing the need for a personal relationship with Him. As a teenager, Ken turned from church to drinking and experimenting with drugs. In high school, a family with whom his best friend was living invited them both to go to church. At the meeting, in order to please his friend, Ken pretended to accept Christ, was baptized, and returned home enthused enough that he invited his sister to accompany him to church. Because of an unfortunate experience involving his sister and a church leader, Ken left the church and never returned.

Returning to drinking and drugs, Ken soon met and married a young lady from the restaurant where he worked. They had a son named Kyle, and continued to drink and take drugs. Ken was, however, shocked into reality and admitting the seriousness of his condition when, while drinking one night, he nearly put baby Kyle into a tub of scalding water.

After some initial success with the Alcoholics Anonymous (AA) program, Ken returned to drinking and came home one night to find that his wife and son had left. As a condition of staying together, Ken returned to AA. At the January 15, 1987 meeting, he gave up drinking forever after being challenged by the group's leader to turn away from alcohol in order to reclaim his life and family. As he studied the twelve-step program, the concept of a higher power kept going through Ken's mind, but because the memory of his sister's church experience had left him bitter toward Christian leadership, he and his wife pursued Judaism instead.

For the next fourteen years, Ken remained closed to anything related to Jesus Christ. During that time, he got divorced, remarried, and divorced again. He also became involved in the Sterling Institute of Relationship, a humanistic men's accountability group.

In 2000, Ken met Dana Prevost, a Christian fireman, and while catering a wedding reception for Dana's daughter, he met Mike Boone, a successful local businessman. During the toast to the bride and his son the groom, Mike shared how he and his wife had been on the brink of divorce and only rescued their marriage by turning their relationship over to Jesus Christ. He admonished the newlyweds to begin married life on the right foot, or rather, the rock—the solid rock of Jesus.

Ken was so moved by this commitment to the Jesus from whom he'd been running all these years, that he spoke with Mike at length during the party. Mike even prayed with him at the table.

It's important that I be accountable to others

The next day, not coincidentally, Ken and I (Roy), while having coffee at a local coffeehouse, were introduced by a mutual friend, Howard Flaherty. After Ken shared with us a bit about his past involvement with the Sterling Institute's men's accountability groups, I invited him to join our newly formed TriCord—an accountability group with a Biblical foundation.

Initially, Ken was guarded, he didn't want to be disappointed like he had been in the past, but he persisted. We even got to spend some one-on-one time together discussing Jesus' claims about who he is and how he wants to have a life-changing relationship with his people. After having to drop out of the group in order to pursue a burgeoning catering business, and being plagued by doubts about Jesus' claim to be the only way to eternal life, Ken returned to his TriCord. It was at that time that Jeff Steele recommended that Ken read Lee Strobel's book, The Case For Christ._To my surprise, he went right out and bought the book. That very afternoon he called me, excitedly declaring, "This book answers every one of my questions." His question about there being Biblical truths in all religions was also answered.

At the next TriCord meeting, Ken shared how, after reading Lee's book, he was now convinced that the Bible and Jesus Christ were real and true. But because Ken felt that there was too much sin in his life, he just couldn't accept Jesus as Savior.

After I talked to Ken about Jesus' desire to forgive sin; His desire to help His sons and daughters to walk in freedom, healing, and joy; and His power to heal our past, Ken went home. A few days later, we met for breakfast and he proudly exclaimed, "Can't you tell?" "Can't I tell what?" I asked. "That I opened my heart to Jesus and He came in."

The next week, Ken shared his new faith in Christ with the men in his TriCord, and he continues to influence men both inside and outside his group who have not yet accepted Christ as their Savior. In fact, Ken now attends two TriCords and leads a third. He also speaks at the local jails where men readily identify with his search for the truth and, as a result, accept Jesus as their Lord and Savior.

In conclusion:

> Being a believer, you know Christ as your personal Lord and Savior. The peace that you receive from knowing that you will live in God's presence for all eternity and

that your sins are forgiven is reflected in the way you live your life. The world around you sees that there is something different about you. But, even though they may not know what it is, they want what they see in your life. As a believer, it is your privilege to share Christ as the source of your peace. You should desire to know Christ so well that others will be able to see His likeness in you.

I know Christ so well that others see His likeness in me

Chapter Two

ETERNAL LIFE IS A FREE GIFT

Questions for home study and group discussion

What do our hearts and mouths have to do with our salvation? Romans 10:8-10, 13

Is trusting in Christ by faith enough for God to save us? Explain.
Romans 3:24-25a

What should we do now that God has saved us from sin's death penalty? Romans 5:11

What eternal assurance do we have that we will go to Heaven? I John 5:11-13

Is there anything we can do to earn our place in Heaven? Ephesians 2:8-9

My Personal Testimony

(Write out your testimony of how Christ changed your life.)

What I was like before Christ

How I came to Christ

How my life has changed after I received Christ

Scripture Memory Chapter Two

"And this is the testimony that God gave us eternal life, and this life is in his Son. Whoever has the Son has life; whoever does not have the Son of God does not have life. I write these things to you who believe in the name of the Son of God that you may know that you have eternal life." (I John 5:11-13)

Characteristic Two

BEING EMPOWERED

I AM CONTROLLED AND
EMPOWERED BY THE HOLY SPIRIT

Chapter Three THE HOLY SPIRIT IS GOD

Chapter Four OBEY THE HOLY SPIRIT

Chapter Three

THE HOLY SPIRIT IS GOD

"But I say, walk by the Spirit, and you will not gratify the desires of the flesh." (Galatians 5:16)

The second spiritual characteristic, being empowered, is having the power to live Christ-like. As believers, we continue to have freedom of choice. We have settled the issue of heaven and hell. But now, we must choose daily whether or not we will live to satisfy the flesh or the Spirit.

We can decide whether or not we will live Christ-like or just drift through life walking after the things of this world. When we don't walk in the Spirit, we end up feeling abandoned and alone. The choice is up to us, we can either put in the effort to be Christ-like or just let life happen.

There are two identical homes. Both have the same upgrades and are even on the same street. They are identical in every way, but one—their owners. One house has a family that cares for it; they take their shoes off before entering, they are diligent cleaners and take pride in how the house looks inside and out. On the contrary, the other house has a family that does not take the time to keep it looking nice. The kids track mud throughout the house, the paint is peeling and their neighbors are complaining because of all the weeds in the yard. Unfortunately, this family does not put forth the time or effort it takes to maintain a beautiful home. The difference in the houses' condition is completely dependent on the diligence of their owners. Likewise, our spiritual condition reflects our diligence in following Christ.

When Jesus told Nicodemus, "You must be born again," He didn't mean we would get rid of our bodies. We were born spiritually. Our soul and spirit operate together within our bodies. We already mentioned earlier that God has given us free will—the ability to choose. So now our soul is a battlefield between two very strong powers. Satan tries to use the soul to satisfy our sinful cravings. Satan knows this is the greatest form of control he has. Since he no longer has any eternal hold on us, Satan will do all he can to keep us from glorifying Christ by keeping us bound in our own sin.

Somewhere between conception and birth, we were given a soul. Our soul is made up of the mind, the will, and the emotions. We also know that we will live forever because we possess a soul and spirit. As natural human beings, our souls strive to satisfy the desires of the flesh. Without Christ and the indwelling of the Holy Spirit, all a person can do is continually look for ways to fulfill the needs and pleasures of the flesh.

As humans, we draw upon our mind, our will, and our emotions to satisfy these cravings. The difference between love and lust is that love is easily satisfied, but lust is insatiable. I John 2:16 in the Living Bible defines lust in three ways:

- The craze for sex
- The ambition to buy everything that appeals to you
- The pride that comes from wealth and importance

Satan, the prince and ruler of this world (Ephesians 2:2), uses our drive to satisfy the pleasures of the flesh in order to control us. He deceives us into believing that we are happy and successful when we attain all this world has to offer. Jesus said, "That which is born of the flesh is flesh, and that which is born of the Spirit is spirit." (John 3:6) He also said, *"Do not marvel that I said to you, 'You must be born again."* (John 3:7)

I have the power to live Christ-like

Until this new birth took place, we were only functioning in the flesh and were dead spiritually under the dictates of Satan. Satan was our father (John 8:44). We had no choice but to do what he wanted us to do. God's Word says, *"But to all who did receive him, who believed in his name, he gave the right to become children of God, who were born, not of blood nor of the will of the flesh nor of the will of man, but of God."* (John 1:12-13)

God is Spirit and must be worshipped in spirit (John 4:24). Before this spiritual birth, we could not worship and obey God; we could not communicate with Him. However, now that we are born into His family, as His children, we can turn to Him for guidance. God our Heavenly Father loves us with an unconditional love and wants to teach us how to please Him. *"Therefore, if anyone is in Christ, he is a new creation. The old has passed away; behold, the new has come."* (II Corinthians 5:17)

God, my Heavenly Father, loves me with an unconditional love

The Holy Spirit wants to work through our soul and spirit to give us victory over the flesh. Praise the Lord, He did not leave us alone in the struggle! Before Jesus went to heaven to be with the Father, He promised to send us a comforter, the Holy Spirit. But who is the Holy Spirit?

God manifests Himself in three separate persons: God the Father, God the Son, and God the Holy Spirit. That is where the word trinity comes from. The Holy Spirit is the third member of the Trinity. There are three characteristics that only God possesses: God is omnipotent, omniscient, and omnipresent. All three characteristics are attributed to the Holy Spirit, showing that the Holy Spirit is God.

These attributes prove that the Holy Spirit is God

The Holy Spirit is omnipotent - all-powerful. In Luke, the angel, talking to Mary the mother of Jesus answered her, *"The Holy Spirit will come upon you, and the power of the Most High will overshadow you; therefore, the child to be born will be called holy—the Son of God."* (Luke 1:35) When the Holy Spirit came upon Mary, it was the power of the Most High. This means that His power is equal to the power of God, because He is God.

The Holy Spirit is omniscient - all-knowing. In First Corinthians, Paul says, *"These things God has revealed to us through the Spirit. For the Spirit searches everything, even the depths of God."* (I Corinthians 2:10) In order for the Holy Spirit to know all of the depths of God, the Holy Spirit must be all-knowing. This means He knows all the deepest secrets of God, because He is God.

The Holy Spirit is omnipresent - ever-present. David proclaims, "Where shall I go from your Spirit? Or where shall I flee from your presence?" (Psalm 139:7) The Psalmist goes on to say that no matter where he would go, high in the Heavens, low down into hell, to the uttermost parts of the sea, to the right or the left, in the darkness or the light, the Holy Spirit is everywhere. The Holy Spirit was also present at the creation. In Genesis it says, *"The earth was without form and void, and darkness was over the face of the deep. And the*

Spirit of God was hovering over the face of the waters." (Genesis 1:2) In other words, the Holy Spirit is ever-present. This means He is everywhere at the same time. He has always been and always will be, because He is God.

> "The Holy Spirit is God, and equal to the Father and the Son. We should not speak of Him as an "it" or refer to Him as an influence. He is God the Holy Spirit, and is set forth in the Bible as being distinct from the Father and the Son. When David sinned against the Lord, he prayed *"Cast me not away from your presence, and take not your Holy Spirit from me."* (Psalm 51:11) In the New Testament after Pentecost, we see the Holy Spirit indwelling the believer, never to leave us, filling and empowering us for service." (The Open Bible, reference page 879).

JESUS PROMISED TO SEND A HELPER

Jesus said,

> *And I will ask the Father, and he will give you another Helper. He will be with you forever, even the Spirit of truth, whom the world cannot receive, because it neither sees him nor knows him. You know him, for he dwells with you and will be in you. "I will not leave you as orphans; I will come to you. Yet a little while and the world will see me no more, but you will see me.*

The Holy Spirit leads me into all truth

> *Because I live, you also will live. In that day you will know that I am in my Father and you in me, and I in you. These things I have spoken to you while I am still with you. But the Helper, the Holy Spirit, whom the Father will send in my name, he will teach you all things and bring to your remembrance all that I have said to you. (John 14:16-20, 25-26)*

The power of the life giving Spirit is mine in Christ Jesus

Have you ever thought of how great it would be if Jesus were here with us every day in the flesh, just as He was with the disciples? Then we could really live the Christian life. We would have Him here as our example. We would have Him here to teach us and show us His miracles. Wow! Then we could make it. We would be terrific Christians wouldn't we? Jesus said, *"Nevertheless, I tell you the truth: it is to your advantage that I go away, for if I do not go away, the Helper will not come to you. But if I go, I will send him to you."* (John 16:7)

> *"until the day when he was taken up, after he had given commands through the Holy Spirit to the apostles whom he had chosen And while staying with them he ordered them not to depart from Jerusalem, but to wait for the promise of the Father, which, he said, "you heard from me; for John baptized with water, but you will be baptized with the Holy Spirit not many days from now."* (Acts 1:2, 4-5, 8)

> *"When the day of Pentecost arrived, they were all together in one place. And suddenly there came from heaven a sound like a mighty rushing wind, and it filled the entire house where they were sitting. And divided tongues as of fire appeared to them and rest on each one of them. And they were all filled with the Holy Spirit and began to speak in other tongues as the Spirit gave them utterance." (Acts 2:1-4 TLB)*

I have been filled with the Holy Spirit

Paul knew that when we receive Christ, we also receive the Holy Spirit. He knew that the Holy Spirit seals us into Christ at the time of the new birth (II Corinthians 1:22). However, we are then baptized with the Holy Spirit when we decide by an act of our will to ask the Holy Spirit to completely take control of our body, our soul, and our spirit. It is this complete submission of ourselves to the Holy Spirit that gives us the power to walk in the Spirit instead of walking in the flesh.

BECAUSE OF CHRIST I HAVE THE HOLY SPIRIT'S POWER OVER THE FLESH

> *"For God has done what the law, weakened by the flesh, could not do. By sending his own Son in the likeness of sinful flesh and for sin, he condemned sin in the flesh, in order that the righteous requirement of the law might be fulfilled in us, who walk not according to the flesh but according to the Spirit. For those who live according to the flesh set their minds on the things of the*

> *flesh, but those who live according to the Spirit set their minds on the things of the Spirit. For to set the mind on the flesh is death, but to set the mind on the Spirit is life and peace. For the mind that is set on the flesh is hostile to God, for it does not submit to God's law; indeed, it cannot. Those who are in the flesh cannot please God. You, however, are not in the flesh but in the Spirit, if in fact the Spirit of God dwells in you. Anyone who does not have the Spirit of Christ does not belong to him."* *(Romans 8:2-9)*

I CHOOSE TO WHOM I WILL YIELD CONTROL OF MY LIFE

A story appeared in a Time Magazine article a number of years ago about a man who possessed a family heirloom - a large rock that was used as a paperweight. One day, the rock dropped off his desk and split open. To make a long story short, inside that paperweight was a rough diamond. When the diamond was cut and polished it was around 80 karats.

Although the man had actually possessed the priceless jewel his whole life, the question becomes, "When did he actually know he was rich?" Was he rich all along or was it only when he discovered what he really possessed?

> *I no longer obey the old evil nature within me*

When we surrender ourselves to the control of the Holy Spirit, we receive the power to live the life Christ intends for us. When we were baptized with the Holy Spirit, we gave Him complete control. Like the family heirloom, it's then when we become fully aware of the richness of God's gift. Being baptized, fully surrendered, or dead to our "old self" makes us new daily.

We know we have the ability, even though we are believers, to seek ways to satisfy the desires of our flesh. When we do this, we break fellowship with our Heavenly Father. God loves us and refuses to make robots out of us. He gives us the freedom each day to choose whether we are going to please the flesh or the Spirit. When we do not follow the Holy Spirit's guidance and depend on our human abilities, we get into trouble. God tells us that we can ask the Holy Spirit for daily instructions and He will lead us. Because we will always act out what we really believe, we can know if we are yielding to the Spirit or to the flesh by the kind of behavior we manifest.

This may be why the Bible says that you shall know them by their fruit. It is true that we are not saved by what we do. It is also true that if we are really saved, our actions will reflect the change that takes place in our hearts when Christ enters. If a man continues to behave as the world does, then what he says is not necessarily a reflection of what he really believes. For his actions speak so loud that we can't hear what he is saying. If he has truly accepted Christ, his life will change as he endeavors to conform to the image of Christ.

My actions reflect the change that took place in my heart when Christ entered

Even as believers, however, we may give into the flesh and allow Satan to control us. When we are walking in the flesh, our lives will reflect certain worldly behavior, and when we walk in the Spirit we will reflect certain Godly behavior. We will always bear fruit, whether it is the fruit of the Spirit or of the flesh. We must monitor the fruit that our own lives produce. The fruit that is coming from my own life will tell me if I am really following after the Holy Spirit or after the flesh.

Chapter Three

THE HOLY SPIRIT IS GOD

Questions for home study and group discussion

What does it mean to be Omnipotent?
Luke 1:35

What does it mean to be Omnipresent?
Psalms 139:7, Genesis 1:2

What does it mean to be Omniscient?
I Corinthians 2:10

Based on your answers above, who is the Holy Spirit?

What is the Holy Spirit's primary responsibility?
John 14:25-26

Notes from My Mentor's Personal Experiences

Scripture Memory Chapter Three

"But I say, walk by the Spirit, and you will not gratify the desires of the flesh." (Galatians 5:16)

Chapter Four

OBEY THE HOLY SPIRIT

"But the fruit of the Spirit is love, joy, peace, patience, kindness, goodness, faithfulness, gentleness, self-control; against such things there is no law." (Galatians 5:22-23)

A man had a precious singing bird who visited his home daily. After a number of years, this beautiful, brightly colored bird was a source of joy and inspiration. The songs and peaceful nature of this creature often settled broken hearts, quelled household disputes, and calmed anxious spirits. Not only was it now considered a family member, but neighbors and others outside of the community now shared the family's joy.

One day, on his way home from work, that same man saw a cute little puppy in his neighborhood. No one actually owned the dog, so the man began to occasionally feed him. Eventually, the puppy grew and began to take shape into an unattractive, muscular creature displaying occasional viciousness. It was constantly causing problems on his street.

Having grown quite fond of this little troublemaker, the man took the dog into his home.

The man continued to feed the dog, and it grew to be mean and territorial about the man's home, yard, and even the man himself. Family members were the first to complain; yet he persisted in loving the dog, which began to not only damage the furniture and soil the carpets, but also nip at other family members and neighbors.

Soon after the man brought the dog into his home, the precious singing bird left and rarely was seen. Now, not only was there a sense of loss but in its place a continuous barking. The man's home was in an uproar. The source of unrest and aggravation was the dog. It grew strong, mean, and dominant. The man could barely leave his own home. His family was in fear.

It was time to act! But as the man wrestled to take the dog out of the home, it mauled him. Perplexed, the man realized his little pet now controlled his home and soon threatened to drive away his own family.

We have a struggle between the flesh and the spirit. The spirit calls on the soul to satisfy the needs of the Spirit. Now our mind, will, and emotions are expected to seek out ways of pleasing the spirit. However, our spirit can only be satisfied when it is under the control of God the Holy Spirit. When Paul said, "*We are to walk in the Spirit, not in the flesh,*" (Galatians 5:16) he was referring to this commitment of the mind, the will, and the emotions to the Holy Spirit. He also said that it is God's purpose for believers to "*be conformed to the image of His Son*" (Romans 8:29). The word "image" means to become like or take on the likeness of something or someone else. We are

I obey the Holy Spirit's instructions. He tells me where to go and what to do.

to become the likeness of Christ. The living Christ is to be reflected through our lives.

Jesus is our example. He always reflected God the Father's image. Throughout Christ's life, we see that it was His desire to do the Father's will, not the will of the flesh; even when it meant suffering death on the cross. (Matthew 26:39, 42) Jesus prayed to God the Father for His disciples:

> *"I have given them your word, and the world has hated them because they are not of the world, just as I am not of the world. I do not ask that you take them out of the world, but that you keep them from the evil one. They are not of the world, just as I am not of the world. Sanctify them in the truth; your word is truth. As you sent me into the world, so I have sent them into the world." (John 17:14-18)*

As a believer, I am in the world, but not of the world

As a believer, you are in the world, but you are not part of the world. You are a child of God. You are a citizen of Heaven. You are Christ's ambassador here in this world reconciling it to God.

> *"Do not love the world or the things in the world. If anyone loves the world, the love of the Father is not in him. For all that is in the world—the desires of the flesh and the desires of the eyes and pride of life—is not from the Father but is from the world. And the world is passing away along with*

> *its desires, but whoever does the will of God abides forever." (I John 2:15-17)*

"Do not be conformed to this world but be transformed by the renewal of your mind, that by testing you may discern what is the will of God, what is good and acceptable and perfect." (Romans 12:2) Believers need a different definition of failing and succeeding than what the world suggests. To us, failure and success must relate to the degree with which we (1) walk in the flesh, satisfying the desires of the flesh with the customs and behavior of this world, or (2) walk in the Spirit, obeying the will of God while conforming to the image of His Son.

> *I do not copy the behavior and customs of this world*

THE INTENT OF OUR HEARTS IS MANIFESTED THROUGH OUR ACTIONS

> *"But I say, walk by the Spirit, and you will not gratify the desires of the flesh. For the desires of the flesh are against the Spirit, and the desires of the Spirit are against the flesh, for these are opposed to each other, to keep you from doing the things you want to do. But if you are led by the Spirit, you are not under the law." (Galatians 5:16-18)*

The Bible gives us a good test to determine whether or not we are living according to the flesh or the Spirit. Study carefully how the following Scriptures in Galatians 5 Verses 19-20 show the evidence of sin in our lives. They reveal to us that we are living in the flesh instead of the Spirit. If you have the things that are listed under the "Works of the Flesh," ask

God to forgive you and commit yourself to apply the things listed under "Fruits of the Spirit." The items under this second category, verses 22-24, are natural results of being obedient to the Holy Spirit and indicate that your life is under His control.

WORKS OF THE FLESH

> *"Now the works of the flesh are evident: sexual immorality, impurity, sensuality, idolatry, sorcery, enmity, strife, jealousy, fits of anger, rivalries, dissensions, divisions, envy, drunkenness, orgies, and things like these. I warn you, as I warned you before, that those who do such things will not inherit the kingdom of God." (Galatians 5:19-21)*

I walk in the Spirit, not in the flesh

FRUITS OF THE SPIRIT

> *"But the fruit of the Spirit is love, joy, peace, patience, kindness, goodness, faithfulness, gentleness, self-control; against such things there is no law. And those who belong to Christ Jesus have crucified the flesh with its passions and desires." (*Galatians 5:22-24)

In verse 22, the Living Bible says: *"But when the Holy Spirit controls our lives He will produce this kind of fruit in us."* The Holy Spirit develops the fruits of the Spirit as we give Him control. We cannot develop these attributes on our own.

HOW DO WE RECEIVE THE HOLY SPIRIT AND GIVE HIM CONTROL?

Following are three ways that the Holy Spirit enters, controls, and empowers our lives.

1 The Holy Spirit enters our lives when we receive Christ

When the new birth takes place, the Holy Spirit seals the believer into Christ. *"and who has also put his seal on us and given us his Spirit in our hearts as a guarantee"* (II Corinthians 1:22) He immerses us into or saturates us with the person of Christ. He takes all of our sin and puts it in Christ and takes all of Christ's righteousness and puts it in us. *"For our sake he made him to be sin who knew no sin, so that in him we might become the righteousness of God."* (II Corinthians 5:21) We are brought into right standing with God, our Heavenly Father. The Holy Spirit seals our position in the family of God. "*And do not grieve the Holy Spirit of God, by whom you were sealed for the day of redemption.*" (Ephesians 4:30) We are born spiritually and will live for all of eternity, never to be separated from the love of God. (Romans 8:31-39)

2. The Holy Spirit takes control of our lives when we ask Him

The Holy Spirit must control our lives in order for us to live the holy life that God intended for each believer. Just as Jesus does not force Himself on a person, but allows them to invite Him into their life by an act of their free will, so the Holy Spirit does not force His control over the believer. Even

> *I have nailed my natural evil desires to His cross*

though we have the Holy Spirit living in us at the time of the new birth (Romans 8:9), He does not take control of our life unless we surrender that control to Him. When we surrender every area of our life to the control of the Holy Spirit, He takes control. In this way, we are baptized with the Holy Spirit. We are completely surrendered to Him.

3. The Holy Spirit empowers us daily as we yield control of our lives to Him.

The Holy Spirit sealed my position in the family of God

Because we still live in this body of flesh, it is natural for us to desire the things of this world. It is only through a daily awareness of the Holy Spirit's control that we are empowered to live Christ-like; the way God intends. Each day we need to be emptied of self and filled with the Holy Spirit. When we were baptized with the Holy Spirit, we made a commitment to give Him complete control.

Being filled or empowered with the Holy Spirit is a daily reminder of that commitment. It is like spiritual breathing. As we daily confess our sins to the Father, we invite the Holy Spirit to continue His control over our lives. Confession is like breathing out the old carbon dioxide. The filling of the Holy Spirit is like breathing in the fresh air. If one is saturated with the Word of God, it makes spiritual breathing so much easier. We are empowered with the Holy Spirit when we recognize His complete control of our lives each day. The Word of God commands us to be filled with the Holy Spirit (Ephesians 5:18).

ASK THE HOLY SPIRIT TO CONTROL AND EMPOWER YOU

The Holy Spirit gives us the power to speak out boldly of Christ's love (Acts 1:8). He teaches us through God's Word how to live Christ-like. He empowers us to resist Satan daily. He gives us special spiritual gifts with which we can worship Him and serve and edify the Body of Christ within the local church. If you have not prayed and asked the Holy Spirit to take control of your life, you can do it now.

The Holy Spirit controls and empowers me

Tell Him that you surrender your flesh, mind, will, and emotions to His complete control. Ask Him to empower you to live your life to glorify God at all times. When you asked Jesus to come into your life to give you eternal life, He came in. So now, when you ask the Holy Spirit to take control and empower you, He will do it also. This is not based on feelings. Jesus promised to give you the Holy Spirit's power so, when you ask Him to take control of and empower you, He will do it in obedience to God's Word.

As a believer, you are completely controlled and empowered by the Holy Spirit. The power and presence of the Holy Spirit in your life will allow you to reflect the likeness of Christ to the world around you. Those who choose to emulate you will emulate the Christ who is exemplified through you by the Holy Spirit's power.

Chapter Four

OBEY THE HOLY SPIRIT

Questions for home study and group discussion

Why should we stop loving this evil world?
I John 2:15-17

How does the Holy Spirit help us live holy lives?
Romans 8:1-2

Can we trust the Holy Spirit to control our lives?
Galatians 5:16 (explain)

What characteristics are reflected in our lives when we are walking in the flesh? Galatians 5:19-21

What characteristics are reflected in our lives when we are controlled by the Holy Spirit? Galatians 5:22-24

Notes from My Mentor's Personal Experience

Scripture Memory Chapter Four

"But the fruit of the Spirit is love, joy, peace, patience, kindness, goodness, faithfulness, gentleness, self-control; against such things there is no law." (Galatians 5:22-23)

Characteristic Three

BEING VICTORIOUS

I HAVE CHRIST'S AUTHORITY
OVER ALL THE ENEMY'S POWER

CHAPTER FIVE

SUBMIT TO GOD AND RESIST THE DEVIL

"Submit yourselves therefore to God. Resist the devil, and he will flee from you." (James 4:7)

The third spiritual characteristic of a Godly life, being victorious, is walking in victory over sin. Most believers have a struggle every day, fighting the battle against the many temptations that come their way. We need to demonstrate our victory and disciple others so they can have victory over sin in their daily lives. We can only do that if we know through God's Word how to have daily victory over sin and temptation in our own lives.

One of the most prestigious and powerful fighting forces in the world is the Navy SEALS. These highly trained and seasoned fighters are able to strike devastating blows to enemy strongholds deep in their own territory. SEAL teams know who the enemy is and how the opposition operates. Each SEAL team carries a powerful array of the most advanced weaponry and communications. Each SEAL team member is capable of using a variety of weapons with exacting precision under the most intense and dangerous conditions. Like a Navy SEAL, we need to know who our enemy is and how to defeat him.

Satan is a powerful spirit and it is important that we know about him. He is evil and is our enemy. Any experience of sin and failure in our lives is due, in part, to his intervention and deception. He uses all of his power every day to try and stop believers from conforming to the image of Christ.

I have daily victory over sin and temptation

He does this because he knows that while we are under the control of the Holy Spirit, we will reveal Christ's love to this dying world. When the world sees the love of Christ in us, they are drawn by the Holy Spirit to desire this love for themselves. Satan does everything he can to blind the world so that people can't see Christ in us. One of the ways he does this is to watch us closely. He assigns his demons to watch us, to catch us off guard.

Satan is not omnipotent, omnipresent, or omniscient. He must have his demons observe our behavior in order to see where we are, how to tempt us, and report our behavior to him. He knows that our behavior will reflect our character. So they watch to see what we really believe by what we do. When his demons see us go to a place or act in a certain way that is not consistent with our commitment as a believer, he attacks. However, he is too intelligent to come on too strong in the beginning. He knows that to get a committed believer to turn away from his desire to daily conform to the image of Christ, he must be very subtle.

SATAN TRIES TO KEEP US AWAY FROM GOD'S WORD

I reveal Christ's love to this dying world

Satan watches us to see in what areas we are most vulnerable. He then puts the things that tempt us within our reach. He knows that if he can keep the things that we are most likely to give into constantly in front of us, he can eventually lead us into sin.

A friend of mine, I'll call him Bob, recently had a satellite dish put on the roof of his house so that he could get twelve sports channels. He was excited about his ability to watch as many NFL games as he wanted to each weekend. However, he soon discovered that with the twelve sports channels came several adult channels. At first, he thought that he would not have a problem with these channels. However, one day, he was surfing through the many channels when he came to a very graphic, erotic act of pornography. He immediately changed the channel. The images, however, stayed in his mind. He soon found himself going back for another look. The temptation got so strong that he found himself lying next to his wife at night waiting for her to go to sleep so that he could slip downstairs in order to watch more pornography.

On that same note, ladies can just as easy fall into a similar trap. Joan was taking her kids to the park where she met Paul, a stay-at-home dad. Their conversation came easily and they enjoyed talking to each other. She gave him good advice about how to get his two-year-old to eat his vegetables and he understood how hard she works during the day. Soon they found themselves practically pushing their spouses out the door in the morning so they could meet at the park. They had invited the enemy into their life and the enemy's plan was working.

Satan will always put the thing that is hardest for you to resist in front of you if you allow him to do so. We do the same things repeatedly until we start believing they're not so bad. "Certainly, God understands that I still love Him. After all, I'm not as bad as some of the people I know," is how we rationalize sin. However, the condemnation and shame cause us to withdraw from our Heavenly Father and other godly fellowship that feeds our spirit.

I do not allow Satan to get me away from God's Word, prayer, and fellowship

The first thing Satan does is to get us away from God's Word, prayer, and fellowship with other believers. Because he knows that, more than anything else, these positive influences are reinforcements in our lives that will keep us on guard against sin. You've heard the saying, "the Bible will keep you away from sin or sin will keep you away from the Bible." There is a great deal of truth to that statement.

In order to resist Satan, we must plan what we are going to do before the temptation is put in front of us. When Jesus was tempted in the wilderness, He was prepared to withstand Satan's temptations in the same way we must be prepared. Jesus answered every temptation with the Word of God. We will study how Jesus did this in chapter eleven. However, a practical way of doing this is to plan ahead.

Most of us know the areas that we are most tempted in; sexual immorality, impure thoughts, alcohol and drugs, lying, stealing, etc. One of the men that I have a mentoring relationship with told me what he does when he travels away from home. Those of us who travel a great deal know that many of the hotels that we stay in usually have a mini-bar. My friend told me that he had trouble resisting the temptation to drink all the alcohol in the mini-bar. Sometimes he would stay up all hours of the night drinking until it began to affect his job performance.

Finally, he submitted to God and made a commitment to the Lord that he was going to get this matter under control. First, he asked God to forgive him for his participation in this sin. He then asked the Holy Spirit to take control over his fleshly desires. After that, he resisted the devil by putting a plan into effect that when he checked into a hotel, he had the hotel take all of the alcohol out of the mini-bar before he went into the room. This way, he was no longer tempted to give into his fleshly desires, and he got victory over this temptation. We all need to take action in the areas of our particular temptations. We must plan ahead for what we will do when the temptation is put in front of us.

God personally picks me up, and sets me firmly in place, and makes me stronger than ever

> *"Be sober-minded; be watchful. Your adversary the devil prowls around like a roaring lion, seeking someone to devour. Resist him, firm in your faith, knowing that the same kinds of suffering are being experienced by your brotherhood throughout the world. And after you have suffered a little while, the God of all grace, who has called you to his eternal glory in Christ, will himself restore, confirm, strengthen, and establish you. To him be the dominion forever and ever. Amen."* (I Peter 5:8-11 TLB)

The Living Bible says in verse 11b; *"He personally will come and pick you up, and set you firmly in place, and make you stronger than ever."*

GOD HAS PROVIDED US WITH A WAY TO DEFEAT SATAN

One of the greatest military threats during World War II was the brilliant German General Erwin Rommel. In the movie "Patton" there is a scene were George C. Scott (who portrays American General George S. Patton) is watching his arch enemy Rommel move a number of heavily armored divisions across the North African desert. All at once, Patton orders his ambushing troops to open fire on the unsuspecting enemy. As the devastation begins and it is apparent to the audience that Patton's troops will be victorious, the actor smiles and comments proudly that he knew what his enemy was going to do because he had studied his tactics.

The apostles Paul, James, and Peter use the phrase, "resist the devil." All of them tell us that Satan is a great enemy. But we can have victory over him by resisting the temptation that he puts in our way. In other words, God provides us with a way to defeat Satan in our daily lives. Paul tells us that Satan is organized.

> *"Put on the whole armor of God, that you may be able to stand against the schemes of the devil. For we do not wrestle against flesh and blood, but against the rulers, against the authorities, against the cosmic powers over this present darkness, against the spiritual forces of evil in the heavenly places. Therefore take up the whole armor of God, that you may be able to withstand in the evil day, and having done all, to stand firm."* (Ephesians 6:11-13)

I wear all of God's armor to stand safe against all strategies and tricks of Satan

Satan has a great army of demons and evil spirits. In order for us to defeat him, we must also be organized and have a battle plan. We must have a strategy to defend ourselves from his attacks. We must also know when and how to attack him. God has given us the battle equipment to fight with. We must know how to use it. Within "Spiritual Characteristic Four," we will deal with the area of putting on the full armor of God.

Before we go into battle, we must know who our enemy is and what our chances are for victory. Where did Satan come from? How did he become our enemy? To answer these questions, we need to examine some facts about Satan.

SATAN IS A CREATED BEING

In Ezekiel we read,

> *"Son of man, raise a lamentation over the king of Tyre, and say to him, thus says the Lord GOD: 'You were the signet of Perfection, full of wisdom and perfect in beauty. You were in Eden, the Garden of God; every precious stone was your covering, sardius, topaz, and diamond, beryl, onyx, and jasper, sapphire, emerald, and carbuncle; and crafted in gold were your settings and your engravings. On the day that you were created they were prepared.*
>
> *You were an anointed guardian cherub. I placed you; you were on the holy mountain of God; in the midst of the stones of fire you*

> *walked. You were blameless in your ways from the day you were created, till unrighteousness was found in you. In the abundance of your trade you were filled with violence in your midst, and you sinned; so I cast you as a profane thing from the mountain of God, and I destroyed you, O guardian cherub, from the midst of the stones of fire. Your heart was proud because of your beauty; you corrupted your wisdom for the sake of your splendor. I cast you to the ground; I exposed you before kings, to feast their eyes on you. By the multitude of your iniquities, in the unrighteousness of your trade you profaned your sanctuaries; so I brought fire out from your midst; it consumed you, and I turned you to ashes on the earth in the sight of all who saw you. All who know you among the peoples are appalled at you; you have come to a dreadful end and shall be no more forever.'"* *(Ezekiel 28:12-19)*

Satan was a created being. As a guardian angel, he was an especially anointed archangel with a very high position in Heaven; he also had a free will. He chose to go his own way instead of God's. Ezekiel said that unrighteousness was found in him, and that his great wealth and beauty caused him to sin. Satan was the first sinner. His heart was filled with pride. He also defiled his holiness with lust for gain. He had the ability to choose right from wrong and he chose wrong.

I have the ability to choose right from wrong. I chose right.

Isaiah says,

> *"O Day Star, son of Dawn! How you are cut down to the ground, you who laid the nations low! You said in your heart, 'I will ascend to heaven; above the stars of God I will set my throne on high; I will sit on the mount of assembly in the far reaches of the north; I will ascend above the heights of the clouds; I will make myself like the Most High.' But you are brought down to Sheol, to the far reaches of the pit."* (Isaiah 14:12-15)

SATAN WAS DEFEATED BY ANOTHER ANGEL

The Apostle John said,

> *"Now war arose in heaven, Michael and his angels fighting against the dragon. And the dragon and his angels fought back, but he was defeated, and there was no longer any place for them in heaven. And the great dragon was thrown down, that ancient serpent, who is called the devil and Satan, the deceiver of the whole world—he was thrown down to the earth, and his angels were thrown down with him."* (Revelation 12:7-9)

SATAN IS NOT EQUAL TO GOD

As we look at Satan's past, we can see that he was an angel created by God. He chose to sin by trying to make himself equal with God. His sin of pride got him thrown out of Heaven. Another angel, Michael, fought against him and defeated him and his angels. Satan is not equal, in any way, with God. John tells us, *"Little children, you are from God and have overcome them, for he who is in you is greater than he who is in the world."* (I John 4:4)

God the Father, God the Son, and God the Holy Spirit all dwell within each believer. The very God that created Satan lives in us. Why should we, for even one second, consider Satan to have any power over us? He has already been defeated.

As a believer, God the Father, God the Son, and God the Holy Spirit all dwell within me

SATAN IS NOT EQUAL TO CHRIST

Jesus said, "Now is the judgment of this world; now will the ruler of this world be cast out." (John 12:31) He went on to say, *"I will no longer talk much with you, for the ruler of this world is coming. He has no claim on me."* (John 14:30) Jesus then said, "*concerning judgment, because the ruler of this world is judged."* (John 16:11)

The writer of Hebrews says, *"Since therefore the children share in flesh and blood, he himself likewise partook of the same things, that through death he might destroy the one who has the power of death, that is, the devil."* (Hebrews 2:14)

Chapter Five

SUBMIT TO GOD AND RESIST THE DEVIL

Questions for home study and group discussion

Where did Satan come from?
Ezekiel 28:12-19

How did Satan become our enemy?
Isaiah 14:12-15

Who cast Satan and his angels from Heaven?
Revelation 12:7-9

What has already happened to Satan?
John 16:11

What happened to Satan when Christ died on Calvary?
Hebrews 2:14

Notes from My Mentor's Personal Experiences

Scripture Memory Chapter Five

"Submit yourselves therefore to God. Resist the devil, and he will flee from you." (James 4:7)

CHAPTER SIX

CHRIST GAVE US HIS AUTHORITY

> “Put on the whole armor of God that you may be able to stand against the schemes of the devil.” (Ephesians 6:11)

Because we have Christ in us, by the power of the Holy Spirit, we have available to us the power and authority to stop Satan in his tracks. Jesus said that He gave us His authority over all the power of the enemy.

> *“When he had entered Capernaum, a centurion came forward to him, appealing to him, ‘Lord, my servant is lying paralyzed at home, suffering terribly.’ And he said to him, ‘I will come and heal him’” But the centurion replied, ‘Lord, I am not worthy to have you come under my roof, but only say the word, and my servant will be healed. For I too am a man under authority, with soldiers under me. And I say to one, ‘Go,’ and he goes, and to another, ‘Come,’ and he comes, and to my servant, ‘Do this,’ and*

> *he does it.' When Jesus heard this, he marveled and said to those who followed him, 'Truly, I tell you, with no one in Israel have I found such faith…' And to the centurion Jesus said, 'Go; let it be done for you as you have believed.' And the servant was healed at that very moment."* (Matthew 8:5-10, 13)

The American Heritage Dictionary defines authority as follows:

1. The right and power to command, enforce laws, exact obedience, determine or judge.
2. A person or group invested with this right or power.
3. Power to influence or persuade resulting from knowledge or experience.
4. An authoritative statement or decision that provides adequate grounds for a course of action or that may be taken as precedent.

The word "power" is defined as follows:

1. The ability or capacity to act or to perform effectively.
2. A specific capacity, faculty, or aptitude.
3. Strength or force exerted or capable of being exerted.
4. The ability or official capacity to exercise control: authority.
5. A person, group, or nation having great influence or control over others.

I have Christ's authority over all of the power of the enemy

In Luke 10:19, Jesus gave us authority over all of the power of the enemy, which means that we have the right and power to command, enforce laws, exact obedience, determine or judge Satan. We have the authority to stop Satan's ability or capacity, to act or to perform effectively. In other words, we not only have the ability to resist Satan, but we can also put a halt to his power and ability to perform effectively.

"And Jesus came and said to them, 'All authority in heaven and on earth has been given to me.' (Matthew 28:18) Before He left to return to the Father, Jesus gave His authority to the believers. *'Behold, I have given you authority to tread on serpents and scorpions, and over all the power of the enemy, and nothing shall hurt you.'* (Luke 10:19) We have Christ's authority over all the power of Satan and his demons. Satan and his demons tremble at the name of Jesus. Jesus said, *"And these signs will accompany those who believe: in my name they will cast out demons; they will speak in new tongues;"* (Mark 16:17) The Living Bible says, "*And those who believe shall use my authority to cast out demons.*" "*Satan must be bound before his demons are cast out, just as a strong man must be tied up before his house can be ransacked and his property robbed.*" (Mark 3:27 TLB) We bind Satan by taking authority over all of his power. When we use the name of Jesus, we show Satan that we have Jesus' authority, therefore, he must obey our command.

BELIEVERS MUST NEVER FEAR SATAN

Believers need not live in fear of Satan, *"for God gave us a spirit not of fear but of power and love and self-control."* (II Timothy 1:7) We can walk with authority and power in the name of Jesus. God did not give us a spirit of fear. Fear is a spirit, placed on us by the enemy. It did not come from God. Many of us have been taught that Satan is so powerful we cannot imagine having authority over all of his power. I once heard the following story and it helped me understand how I am to use my authority over Satan's power.

Imagine an old retired man, weak and underweight, perhaps weighing only one hundred pounds. He wanted a job to keep himself busy. So the city hired him to be a crossing guard by the local school. They gave him a vest to wear, a stop sign, and a badge to show that he had the authority to stop traffic. They forgot to tell him that next to the school, there was some heavy construction going on. They were removing big truckloads of concrete. The huge trucks would rumble down the street toward the intersection where the children crossed to go to school. The little man knew that he did not have the strength to stop those trucks himself. However, he did know that he had the authority from the city to tell those drivers to stop. He did this by simply putting up the stop sign. The drivers would recognize his authority and stop their big trucks at his command.

This is the way our authority in Christ works. We do not have the power in ourselves to stop Satan. But when we use the name of Jesus, we are putting up the stop sign and Satan recognizes our authority to stop his attack. We can talk to Satan and his emissaries in the name of Jesus. When he attacks, say, "Satan, I take authority over all your power in the name of Jesus." Let's say that Satan is attacking you with a spirit of fear. You say, "You demon of fear, I take authority over you in the name of Jesus." Satan and his demons must obey your authority over them in the name of Jesus.

God did not give me a spirit of fear but of power, and love, and of a sound mind

SATAN IS A DEFEATED ENEMY

The important thing for us to remember is that Satan is a defeated enemy. He was totally defeated at Calvary. When Jesus died and was buried, He rose again proving His power over sin and death. He purchased us back from Satan. Satan lost his place of dominion over our lives. He now only has the power to influence us if we give it to him. Satan has no right to touch us because we are the property of God, purchased for Him by Christ's blood. Satan cannot cross the bloodline.

"He disarmed the rulers and authorities and put them to open shame, by triumphing over them in him." (Colossians 2:15) *"We know that everyone who has been born of God does not keep on sinning, but he who was born of God protects him, and the evil one does not touch him."* (I John 5:18) Even though Satan knows he has lost the eternal battle for our soul, he will continue to try to get us to sin. However, God gave us the tools to protect ourselves from Satan's attack.

God has shown me how to escape temptation's power

> *"No temptation has overtaken you that is not common to man. God is faithful, and he will not let you be tempted beyond your ability, but with the temptation he will also provide the way of escape, that you may be able to endure it."* (I Corinthians 10:13)

PUT OFF THE OLD SELF AND PUT ON THE NEW SELF

We had the privilege of having Dr. W.P. "Tex" Rutledge, Senior Pastor, Praise Chapel of Santa Clarita, California as our Senior Mentor during our first mentor training. His input was invaluable. He helped us understand how to "put off the old self and put on the new self." Dr. Rutledge gave his insights on the first six chapters of this book, and prepared us to put on the full armor of God as explained in the last six chapters.

I have put off the old self and put on the new self

"This material illustrates and defines the difference between 'putting off the old self' with the 'works of the flesh,' and 'resisting the devil and all his devices.' This truth should lead to putting on the whole armor of God as outlined in Ephesians 6. As I point out in my conclusion, I believe our difficulty in reaching the stage of living out the characteristics of a Godly life is primarily in our "old self" trying to "put on" the armor - when only the "new self" can wear the armor of God. The armor is never used to "put off" the old self with his deeds, but to resist the devil. In fact, the whole idea is comical! A good way to test this truth is to compare the "works of the flesh" with the "armor of God" (compare "contentious, anger, envy" with the "gospel of peace." These are contrary to one another. Therefore, a life of hate, anger, etc., cannot wear "the gospel of peace" and so on).

A believer is empowered and becomes victorious by allowing the Holy Spirit to take control of their walk of faith. He recognizes his power and anointing through the Holy Spirit to resist the devil. The following Scriptures give us divine direction, which leads to ultimate victory in Christ. First of all, we need to understand that as children of God, we are no longer subject to the control of our old nature.

"We were buried therefore with him by baptism into death, in order that, just as Christ was raised from the dead by the glory of the Father, we too might walk in newness of life. If we have been united with him in a death like his, we shall certainly be united with him in a resurrection like his. We know that our old self was crucified with him in order that the body of sin might be brought to nothing, so that we would no longer be enslaved to sin. For one who has died has been set free from sin. Now if we have died with Christ, we believe that we will also live with him. We know that Christ, being raised from the dead, will never die again; death no longer has dominion over him. For the death he died he died to sin, once for all, but the life he lives he lives to God. So you also must consider yourselves dead to sin and alive to God in Christ Jesus.

Let not sin therefore reign in your mortal body, to make you obey its passions. Do not present your members to sin as instruments for unrighteousness, but present yourselves to God as those who have been brought from death to life, and your members to God as instruments for righteousness. For sin will have no dominion over you, since you are not under law but under grace." (Romans 6:4-14)

These words of truth and victory are again emphasized:

> *"But that is not the way you learned Christ - assuming that you have heard about him and were taught in him, as the truth is in Jesus, to put off your old self, which belongs to your former manner of life and is corrupt through deceitful desires, and to be renewed in the spirit of your minds, and to put on the new self, created after the likeness of God in true righteousness and holiness."* (Ephesians 4:20-24)

I have put to death those things of the flesh and lusts

The important thing to realize here is that we put off something that is dead. This is our "old self," the "Adamic" nature that will never be subject to the control of the Spirit of God; and, we put on the "new self" in Christ, created in righteousness and true holiness. This "new self" is the force and power of God's Spirit abiding in us which is able to "resist" the devil - for we "resist" something (or someone) that is "alive."

In the preceding Scriptures, we are never told to resist our old self with its deceitful lusts, but to "put it off!" We are not advised to put off the devil and all his assaults and temptation–but we are admonished to resist him! Jesus did this in the wilderness of temptations. He resisted the devil by quoting the Word and put off his desire and lust for physical satisfaction and spiritual gratification–the desire for personal glory and authority.

"If then you have been raised with Christ, seek the things that are above, where Christ is, seated at the right hand of God. Set your minds on things that are above, not on things that are on earth. For you have died, and your life is hidden with Christ in God. When Christ who is your life appears, then you also will appear with him in glory.

Put to death therefore what is earthly in you: sexual immorality, impurity, passion, evil desire, and covetousness, which is idolatry. On account of these the wrath of God is coming. In these you too once walked, when you were living in them. But now you must put them all away: anger, wrath, malice, slander, and obscene talk from your mouth. Do not lie to one another, seeing that you have put off the old self with its practices and have put on the new self, which is being renewed in knowledge after the image of its creator." (Colossians 3:1-10)

We begin to see and understand the work and ministry of the Holy Spirit.

So, how do we put off the old self and put on the new self? Remember in the third chapter of Colossians we are told to "*set your mind on things above*" and "*put to death your members on the earth*" (verses 2 and 5). Nowhere are we advised to "resist" our "old self and its deeds." Therefore, the "set of the mind" is imperative. In II Corinthians 10:3-5, we read how we can "put off" the works and desires of the flesh:

I have set my mind on things above, not on things on earth

"For though we walk in the flesh, we are not waging war according to the flesh. For the weapons of our warfare are not of the flesh but have divine power to destroy strongholds. We destroy arguments and every lofty opinion raised against the knowledge of God, and take every thought captive to obey Christ,"

I bring every thought captive to the obedience of Christ

Now we enter into the faith where we "resist the devil and he will flee from us!" However, I am convinced that we must first "put off" the old self with its works of the flesh, before we can adequately and victoriously "put on" the armor of God to fight the devil!

The defeat of many Christians lies right here in this truth. They are attempting to use the armor of God without deal-

> ing with their selfish desires and works of the flesh. We are given armor to face the foe - I do not read of any protection or weapon to take care of our backside! We must take care of that which is behind us, the sin which once dominated our lives–but now, Jesus Christ the Lord, by His death, has "condemned sin in the flesh" which delivers us from the control and domination of sin in our lives. So now, through the power of the Spirit, we can "crucify the flesh with the affections and lusts" thereby, "putting off the old self" and "putting on the new self." And the new self puts on and wears the armor of God. The old self cannot put on the armor of a Holy God - it does not fit him or belong to him.
>
> In conclusion, the spiritual characteristics of a Godly life will involve walking in the Spirit, putting off the works of the flesh, and putting on the new self with righteousness and true holiness. The new self is the only one qualified to put on the whole armor of God to stand against or resist the devil, bringing glorious victory in our lives to the honor of Jesus Christ the Lord!

We must know how to have absolute victory over all of Satan's power. We do that by putting off the old self and putting on the new self and accepting Christ's authority and by using His name to stop Satan from defeating us. Christ completely defeated Satan at Calvary. We are to exemplify Christ's victory over all of Satan's power. We do not reflect a spirit of fear, but of power, of love, and of a sound mind.

Chapter Six

CHRIST GAVE US HIS AUTHORITY

Questions for home study and group discussion

Where do we get our authority over Satan's power?
Luke 10:19

How do we get the devil to flee from us?
James 4:7

Who is in us that is greater than Satan?
I John 4:4, 14:20

What did God give us in place of fear?
II Timothy 1:7

What did God do to Satan in front of the whole world?
Colossians 2:15

Notes from My Mentor's Personal Experience

Scripture Memory Chapter Six

"Put on the whole armor of God that you may be able to stand against the schemes of the devil." (Ephesians 6:11)

Characteristic Four

BEING A WARRIOR

I PUT ON ALL OF GOD'S ARMOR IN ORDER TO DEFEAT SATAN

CHAPTER SEVEN

A LIFE OF TRUTH

"And you will know the truth, and the truth will set you free." *(John 8:32)*

The fourth spiritual characteristic of a Godly life has to do with putting on the full armor of God for warfare against Satan and his army. God promised to provide us with a way to keep temptation from becoming so strong that we can't stand against it. He does this by giving us a full set of armor with which we can fight and defeat against Satan's attempt to destroy us.

GOD HAS EQUIPPED US FOR VICTORY IN SPIRITUAL WARFARE

In the previous characteristic, we talked about our enemy, Satan, the devil. But we need to know that he is not alone. He has an entire army of spiritual beings to assist him in his war against the children of God. We see this in Ephesians 6, *"Put on the whole armor of God, that you may be able to stand against the schemes of the devil. For we do not wrestle against flesh and blood, but against the rulers, against the authorities, against the cosmic powers over this present dark-*

ness, against the spiritual forces of evil in the heavenly places." (Ephesians 6:11-12)

Dr. Rutledge taught us to, "*put off the old self*" and "*put on the new self*" so that the new self can "*put on the full armor of God*" in order to stand against the wiles and cunning devices of the devil. Not only does Satan have his own cunning devices, but he also has a very well organized army. Like any army, there are demons with different levels of authority. There are principalities, powers, and rulers of the darkness and spiritual wickedness in high places. This great army of spiritual beings has two primary objectives: to keep us from coming to Christ, and to keep us from becoming like Christ. We need to know that we are in this spiritual warfare whether we like it or not - it comes with the territory.

When you and I became believers in Jesus Christ we automatically declared ourselves enemies of Satan. At that moment, we became soldiers of the cross. If we are going to be victorious in this battle, we must know what battle gear God has provided for us, and we must know how to use it. In the next six chapters, we will be going through spiritual warfare boot camp. I know that many of you have been fighting this war for quite some time. If you have already put on the new self, and are wearing the full armor of God, then you should help others put on and use their weapons of warfare. You should become a leader in this spiritual battle.

I am in this spiritual battle. I am a soldier of the cross of Christ.

> *"Stand therefore, having fastened on the belt of truth, and having put on the breastplate of righteousness, and, as shoes for your feet, having put on the readiness given by the gospel of peace. In all circumstances take*

> *up the shield of faith, with which you can extinguish all the flaming darts of the evil one; and take the helmet of salvation, and the sword of the Spirit, which is the word of God, praying at all times in the Spirit, with all prayer and supplication. To that end keep alert with all perseverance, making supplication for all the saints,"* (Ephesians 6:14-18)

In the above verses, we are shown six pieces of armor that we are to put on in order to defeat Satan in our effort to daily conform to the image of Christ. We are also told where the real battlefield is located.

I defeat Satan in my effort to daily conform to the image of Christ

When we put this equipment on, we become people of purpose portraying God's values to the world around us.

We become people of truth, position, peace, faith, assurance, His Word, and prayer. This comes about as we put on each of the following pieces of the armor daily:

1. The Belt of Truth — A Life of Truth

2. The Breastplate of Righteousness — A Life of Position

3. The Shoes of the Gospel of Peace — A Life of Peace

4.	The Shield of Faith	A Life of Faith
5.	The Helmet of Salvation	A Life of Assurance
6.	The Sword, which is the Word of God	A Life of His Word
7.	The Battlefield, which is Prayer	A Life of Prayer

The whole armor of God that Paul mentions above is absolutely vital to the believer's ability to walk in the Spirit instead of the flesh.

In order to mentor others, we must live a life of truth. The first piece of armor that we are to put on is the Belt of Truth. In the King James Version, it says, "gird your loins." When we hear the word "loin" we think of loin cloth. The loin cloth is used to cover the most delicate and vulnerable part of the body. So, it would seem that for a believer who lacks truth, he would be most vulnerable to Satan's attacks.

SATAN AND THE WORLD ARE NOT SOURCES OF TRUTH

Today's society is filled with sources of information - television, commercials, the Internet, telemarketers, info-mercials, books filled with "psycho-babble," along with dozens of TV and radio talk shows proclaiming their version of the truth. Recent economic events, including the savings and loan debacle of the late 80s to the Dot Com bubble of the 90s to the Enron scandal of the 2000s and the great recession of 2009, to the recent waves of political disgrace. These events confirm the prevailing deceit of our times.

I cannot find truth in this world

We cannot look to this world or the "Prince of this World" as sources of truth. Satan is the father of lies. Jesus said of the unsaved, *"You are of your father the devil, and your will is to do your father's desires. He was a murderer from the beginning, and does not stand in the truth, because there is no truth in him. When he lies, he speaks out of his own character, for he is a liar and the father of lies."* (John 8:44)

Since Satan is the "Prince of this World," we cannot find truth in the world. The world changes the truth into a lie. *"Because they exchanged the truth about God for a lie and worshiped and served the creature rather than the Creator, who is blessed forever! Amen."* (Romans 1:25) You would think that Paul was writing these things now in our present day. One of Satan's biggest lies is the lie of humanism. The humanist religion has taken control of our education system, our media and government, as well as most of the international community. What was once considered good is now bad and what was once bad is now considered good, all because of the humanist movement. Humanists have truly taken the truth of God and turned it into a lie.

The Humanist Manifesto

Following are several excerpts concerning the Humanist Manifesto. The Humanist Manifesto 2000: A Call for a New Planetary Humanism (Subtitled "A Plan for Peace, Dignity, and Freedom in the Global Human Family") written by Paul Kurtz. What the Bible is to Christians, the Humanist Manifesto is to humanists. They promote atheism, evolution, amorality, self-centered man and one-world government.

1. Atheism

"We find insufficient evidence for belief in the existence of a supernatural; it is either meaningless or irrelevant to the question of the survival and fulfillment of the human race. As non-theists, we begin with humans not God, nature not deity. But we can discover no divine purpose or providence for the human species. While there is much that we do not know, humans are responsible for what we are or will become. No deity will save us; we must save ourselves."

2. Evolution

"Humanism believes that man is part of nature and that he has emerged as the result of a continuous process. Holding an organic view of life, humanists find that the traditional dualism of mind and body must be rejected.

Science affirms that the human species is and emerges from natural evolutionary forces. As far as we know, the total personality is a function of the biological organism transacting in a social and cultural context. There is no credible evidence that life survives the death of the body. We continue to exist in our progeny and in the way that our lives have influenced others in our culture."

3. Amorality

"We affirm that moral values derive their source from human experience. Ethics is autonomous and situational, needing no theological or ideological sanction. Ethics stem from human need and interest. To deny this distorts the whole basis of life.

In the areas of sexuality, we believe that intolerant attitudes, often cultivated by orthodox religions and puritanical cultures, unduly repress sexual conduct. Humanists have called for liberation from repressive puritanical codes."

4. Self-Centered Man

"We reject all religious, ideological, or moral codes that denigrate the individual, suppress freedom, dull intellect, dehumanize personality. We believe in maximum individual autonomy consonant with social responsibility. Although science can account for the causes of behavior, the possibilities of individual freedom of choice exist in human life and should be increased.

Women should have the right to control their own bodies. This includes reproductive freedom, voluntary contraception, and abortion. The opportunity for appropriate sexual education should be made available from an early age. This should include responsible sexual behavior, family planning, and contraceptive techniques. We need to transcend the limits of national sovereignty and to develop a new human identity - membership in the planetary community."

5. One-World Government

"We deplore the division of humankind on nationalistic grounds. We have reached a turning point in human history where the best option is to move toward the building of a world community in which all sectors of the human family can participate. Thus, we look to the development of a system of world law and a world order based upon transnational federal government. The world needs at some point in the future to establish an effective World Parliament - and elected representatives based on population - which represents the people, not their governments. We recommend an international system of taxation - this would not be a voluntary contribution but an actual tax."

HUMANISM'S HATE GOD

As in 1933, humanists still believe that rational theism, especially faith in the prayer-hearing God, assumed to love and care for persons, to hear and understand their prayers, and be able to do something about them, is an unproved and outmoded faith. Salvationism, based on mere affirmation, still appears as harmful, diverting people with false hopes of Heaven hereafter. Reasonable minds look to other means for survival.

Promises of immortal salvation or fear of eternal damnation are both illusory and harmful. They distract humans from present concerns, from self-actualization, and from rectifying social injustices. Modern science discredits such historic concepts as the 'ghost in the machine' and the 'separable soul.'"

WHERE DO WE FIND THE TRUTH?

Everything the humanists are teaching is in direct opposition to the Word of God. God has given us the truth. Man, in his wisdom, has changed God's truth into a lie. The Word of God says, *"but for those who are self-seeking and do not obey the truth, but obey unrighteousness, there will be wrath and fury."* (Romans 2:8)

With the advent of Hugh Heffner and "Playboy" magazine, the incredible rise of plastic surgery and our insatiable love of spending has become a philosophy that has not only permeated just about all Americans' thinking, but this selfish mentality is now reflected throughout our society. Instead of "God first" or "family first," men and women take care of "me first."

I always stand up for what I believe

Don't think that just because God has allowed these lies to be propagated, that He will not punish those who continue to do so. The above verse says that God will terribly punish them and that His anger is poured out upon them. We must leave that to God. He will do everything in His own time. Our job is to stand up for what we believe.

The humanists have captured our educational systems, our media, and our government. We can no longer just passively stand by and allow the Humanists to have their way in everything. We must strap on the Belt of Truth and draw a line in the sand.

We have accepted the lies of the humanist very gradually until some of what they teach is starting to make sense to us. We are like the story about the frog that was boiled to death. It is said that if you put a frog in a pot of hot boiling water, he will just jump out. But if you put him in a pot of lukewarm water he will get comfortable and get used to the water. You can then slowly turn up the heat, eventually it will get boiling hot, but the frog will just sit there until he is cooked to death. That is how we have become susceptible to the enemy's lies.

I am not addressing all the issues raised by the Humanist Manifesto. However, this three-book series on "Twelve

Characteristics of a Godly Life" will teach the truth by which we can live our lives in order to conform to the image of Christ, and how to stand against the lies of the enemy and his army of unseen spirits, as well as the humans he has recruited to promote his false agenda. Let's ask the question, "If we cannot find truth in the world, where do we find it?" We will find that there are four primary sources of truth.

FOUR PRIMARY SOURCES OF TRUTH

Truth is found in God the Father, God the Son, God the Holy Spirit, and in God's Word

1. God the Father - *"But the hour is coming, and is now here, when the true worshipers will worship the Father in spirit and truth, for the Father is seeking such people to worship him."* (John 4:23) I am operating under the assumption that you have already accepted the truth that God does exist and that He is who He claims to be in the Bible. In Genesis 1:1, it simply states that, "*In the beginning God.*" God does not try to explain who He is, He just states that He is, and that He created the heavens and the earth. If you accept this premise, then you immediately recognize that what the world is teaching about God is a lie. We learn about God from His Word, as well as by what we see in creation.

> *"For the wrath of God is revealed from heaven against all ungodliness and unrighteousness of men, who by their unrighteousness suppress the truth. For what can be known about God is plain to them, because God has shown it to them. For his invisible attributes, namely, his eternal power and divine nature, have been clearly perceived,*

ever since the creation of the world, in the things that have been made. So they are without excuse. For although they knew God, they did not honor him as God or give thanks to him, but they became futile in their thinking, and their foolish hearts were darkened. Claiming to be wise, they became fools," (Romans 1:18-22)

I know the truth, and the truth has set me free

2. God the Son - *Jesus said to him, "I am the way, and the truth, and the life. No one comes to the Father except through me."* (John 14:6) We have already studied about Jesus and who He claimed to be in Characteristic One. If you have accepted Christ, then it is obvious to you that the world does not understand the truth about Him. The Bible says that Jesus is the Christ, the Messiah, and the Son of God. In fact, it says that He is God. Jesus says that He is the Truth and that the Truth will set you free. So Jesus said to the Jews who had believed him, "If you abide in my word, you are truly my disciples, and you will know the truth, and the truth will set you free." (John 8:31-32)

When you know that you have Christ in your life and that your sins are all forgiven, a great sense of freedom and peace comes into your life. Put your trust in Christ. Be willing to test what He teaches through the Word. If you have any questions about your relationship with Christ, go back to Characteristic One and read it over until you fully understand. If you still have doubts or questions, go to your pastor or a person that you know is a believer and ask for help.

3. God the Holy Spirit - When Jesus promised to send the Holy Spirit, He said, *"When the Spirit of truth comes, he*

will guide you into all the truth, for he will not speak on his own authority, but whatever he hears he will speak, and he will declare to you the things that are to come." (John 16:13) It is the work of the Holy Spirit to teach us and lead us into all truth. Remember, if we allow the Holy Spirit to control and empower us, He will guide us and show us what to do through the Word of God. To review what we learned about the Holy Spirit, go back to Characteristic Two.

I am becoming more like Christ by always speaking and living the truth

4. God's Word - Jesus said to His Father in prayer before His ascension into Heaven, *"Sanctify them in the truth; your word is truth. And for their sake I consecrate myself, that they also may be sanctified in truth."* (John 17:17, 19) We only know God's truth by studying God's Word. Paul tells us to, *"Do your best to present yourself to God as one approved, a worker who has no need to be ashamed, rightly handling the word of truth."* (II Timothy 2:15) We will examine this subject more completely in the chapter on "A Life of His Word." There we will learn how to use the Sword of the Holy Spirit, the Word of God, as a weapon in our warfare against the enemy.

Any time we lie, we are giving into Satan's control. He knows that if he can get us to lie, he will be able to get us away from the Holy Spirit's control. He knows that one lie always seems to need another lie to cover up the first, until we get so used to lying that we lose perspective on the truth. We start justifying our need to tell lies (e.g., Lies are necessary to protect a loved one, etc).

> *"Rather, speaking the truth in love, we are to grow up in every way into him who is the head, into Christ, from whom the whole*

> *body, joined and held together by every joint with which it is equipped, when each part is working properly, makes the body grow so that it builds itself up in love. Therefore, having put away falsehood, let each one of you speak the truth with his neighbor, for we are members one of another." (Ephesians 4:15-16, 25)*

Truth is the first defensive weapon God gave us in order to resist and defeat Satan. We must commit ourselves to live a life of truth by always telling the truth, as well as standing up for the truth. Otherwise, we are giving into Satan, the father of lies. We are allowing him to control us. But as you yield yourselves to the Holy Spirit's control, He will give you the power to speak and live the truth. Remember that He is the "Spirit of Truth." We cannot continue lying and at the same time be under the complete control of the Holy Spirit.

Chapter Seven

A LIFE OF TRUTH

Questions for home study and group discussion

Where is the wrong place to go for truth?
John 8:44, Romans 1:25

List four resources where we find truth.
John 4:23, John 14:17, John 14:6, John 17:17-19

How does God set us free?
John 8:31-32

How does the truth help us grow together to become more like Christ?
Ephesians 4:15-16, 25

How do we show ourselves approved unto God?
II Timothy 2:15

Notes from My Mentor's Personal Experience

Scripture Memory Chapter Seven

"and you will know the truth, and the truth will set you free." (John 8:32)

CHAPTER EIGHT

A LIFE OF POSITION

> *"For our sake he made him to be sin who knew no sin, so that in him we might become the righteousness of God."* (II Corinthians 5:21)

We are people of position in the family of God through Jesus Christ. The second piece of armor is the Breastplate of Righteousness. This protects our heart against the enemy's attack. Our heart is another part of us that is vulnerable. It is the very center of our life. This is the part of us that makes all of the commitments and decisions. Our heart is subject to Satan's attack when it is not protected under the control of the Holy Spirit.

The word righteousness means, "right standing" with God. This, in turn, means to be free from sin. When we receive Jesus Christ as Savior and are born spiritually into God's family, we are placed in a position of right standing with God. Righteousness is not about our behavior. It has to do with our position in Christ. We may not understand the difference between

In Christ, I am a new creature; old things are passed away.

righteousness and holiness. We think that righteousness is the way we behave, but that's not true. Righteousness is what we are in Christ. It has nothing to do with how we act. It is based on what Jesus did for us on the cross in taking away our sin. Righteousness has to do with God's nature that was created in us at the new birth. *"Therefore, if anyone is in Christ, he is a new creation. The old has passed away; behold, the new has come. ...For our sake he made him to be sin who knew no sin, so that in him we might become the righteousness of God."* (II Corinthians 5:17, 21)

If you have Christ as Savior, you are a new creature. Old things have passed away, all things are new, and all things are of God. This new creation is nothing that you did for yourself. It was completely done in you by God. In the above Scripture, we are told that God made Jesus, who knew no sin, to be sin for us that we might be made the righteousness of God in Him. As children of God through Jesus Christ, we are the righteousness of God Himself.

Righteousness is my position in God's family

We are in right-standing with God. When a person accepts Jesus, he enters into the Kingdom of God as God's very own child and a joint heir with Jesus Christ. We didn't get in right-standing with God by being good and behaving right - we got there through faith in Jesus Christ and His redemptive work on the cross. When we accepted the sacrifice of Jesus and invited Him to come into our lives, then God accepted us. Our behavior has unequivocally nothing to do with it.

> *"But now the righteousness of God has been manifested apart from the law, although the Law and the Prophets bear witness to it—the righteousness of God through faith in Jesus Christ for all who believe. For there is*

> *no distinction: for all have sinned and fall short of the glory of God, and are justified by his grace as a gift, through the redemption that is in Christ Jesus, whom God put forward as a propitiation by his blood, to be received by faith. This was to show God's righteousness, because in his divine forbearance he had passed over former sins. It was to show his righteousness at the present time, so that he might be just and the justifier of the one who has faith in Jesus."* (Romans 3:21-26)

Most believers know what they have been saved from, but they don't know about the awesome Kingdom they have been born into. The following are a few verses that may help you understand what Christ's righteousness has done for you. *"He has delivered us from the domain of darkness and transferred us to the kingdom of his beloved Son,"* (Colossians 1:13)

> *"He has now reconciled in his body of flesh by his death, in order to present you holy and blameless and above reproach before him," (Colossians 1:22)*

> *"For you did not receive the spirit of slavery to fall back into fear, but you have received the Spirit of adoption as sons, by whom we cry, "Abba! Father!" The Spirit himself bears witness with our spirit that we are children of God, and if children, then heirs—heirs of God and fellow heirs with Christ, provided we suffer with him in order that we*

may also be glorified with him." (Romans 8:15-17)

WE ARE TO REIGN IN THIS LIFE WITH CHRIST

Righteousness gives you the right to claim your position in God's family. It will enable you to have victory over sin with the knowledge that Satan has already been defeated and has no authority over your life. We are to reign and rule in this life through Jesus Christ. *"For if, because of one man's trespass, death reigned through that one man, much more will those who receive the abundance of grace and the free gift of righteousness reign in life through the one man Jesus Christ."* (Romans 5:17) The above verses tell us that we need to become aware that we have been made the righteousness of God. We have been placed in right-standing with God through the sacrifice of Jesus Christ on the cross. When we do this, we will have the power to stop the continual sin in your life.

The Holy Spirit speaks to me deep in my heart and tells me I really am God's child.

We have been thoroughly equipped to handle every temptation that comes our way. We are to live in daily conformity to the image of Christ, who indwells our hearts by the Holy Spirit, and gives us His righteousness... *"Little children, you are from God and have overcome them, for he who is in you is greater than he who is in the world."* (I John 4:4)

I am awake to my righteousness in Christ and I have victory over sin.

RIGHTEOUSNESS AND HOLINESS

Before we leave this subject, let's take time to consider the difference between righteousness and holiness.

Righteousness is our position in the family of God due to our faith in Jesus Christ. Righteousness is a result of our birth into the family of God just as our physical birth secures our position as a member of our physical family.

We are accepted into the family even though we are only children and do not yet know how to behave as adults.

Righteousness is my position that comes through my faith in Jesus Christ

Righteousness is our position at the time of our spiritual birth. If we have accepted Jesus Christ as our Savior, we are born into the family of God. We are in right-standing with God the Father. We have Christ's righteousness. Our position is settled for all eternity.

Holiness is our pursuit of spiritual maturity. It is our effort to become all that Christ saved us to be. It has to do with the maturing process that takes place as we seek to daily conform to the image of Christ. Holiness is the growth process that charts our development from spiritual childhood. As we learn to walk, we stumble and fall. It is not expected that a newborn baby is capable of walking or communicating as an adult. The goal is to become an adult. No one expects that to happen instantly. It takes time to mature into adulthood.

Holiness is my pursuit of Christ likeness. Holiness comes by my obedience to God's Word

The Holy Spirit is our spiritual parent who guides us in our pursuit of holiness. We make mistakes in our attempt at becoming holy, just as a child fails as he learns to walk. It doesn't mean that the child loses his position in his family just because he fell down when he tried to walk. Some people incorrectly believe that our position in God's family can be taken away because we fail to perform perfectly in our pursuit of spiritual maturity.

If a child is purposely disobedient and does something they know is wrong or displeasing to us, we must discipline them or punish them for their action so that they will learn right from wrong. This is a normal part of the growing process in becoming an adult. But we don't throw the child out of the family. What makes us think that God will throw His children out of His family when they knowingly sin against Him? He will discipline us in order to teach us. God is love. He knows that we will sin and fail many times in our progress toward spiritual maturity. But, He still loves us.

We commit ourselves to the Holy Spirit to parent us in our effort to daily conform to the image of Christ. We will fail over and over in our pursuit of holiness, but we will not lose our position in the family of God.

There is a lot of confusion about the term "backslider." Some people believe that a backslider is a person who was a believer and then did something wrong and, as a result, lost his position in the family of God. Somehow, he became unsaved even though he was once saved.

In contrast, the Bible teaches in the book of Hebrews that a believer who has knowingly disobeyed God is like a disobedient child and needs God the Father's correction.

> *"It is for discipline that you have to endure. God is treating you as sons. For what son is there whom his father does not discipline? If you are left without discipline, in which all have participated, then you are illegitimate children and not sons. Besides this, we have had earthly fathers who disciplined us and we respected them. Shall we not much more be subject to the Father of spirits and live? For they disciplined us for a short time as it seemed best to them, but he disciplines us*

> *for our good, that we may share his holiness. For the moment all discipline seems painful rather than pleasant, but later it yields the peaceful fruit of righteousness to those who have been trained by it."* (Hebrews 12:7-11)

Hopefully, through this discipline, we will learn that God the Father's ways are the right ways, and will submit our will to the control of the Holy Spirit so that we can learn to daily conform to the image of Christ. God says, *"since it is written, 'You shall be holy, for I am holy.'"* (I Peter 1:16) God gives us this command because He knows that it is within our reach if we depend on the Holy Spirit to train us in His ways.

I trust the Holy Spirit to train me in His ways.

In conclusion:

Righteousness is our position that comes through faith in Jesus Christ. Holiness is our pursuit of Christ likeness. Holiness comes by obedience to God's Word.

Putting on the Breastplate of Righteousness is recognizing that you are in the family of God, and knowing that you are in right-standing with God because of your relationship with Jesus Christ. You are a person of position in the Kingdom of God. This knowledge will help you keep this piece of armor firmly in place at all times.

Chapter Eight

A LIFE OF POSITION

Questions for home study and group discussion

As believers, what is our position in God's family?
II Corinthians 5:17, 21

Where does our righteousness come from?
Romans 3:22

What did Christ rescue us from and what are we born into?
Colossians 1:13

How are we to live now that we are in right standing with God?
Romans 8:15-17

Righteousness is my _____________ in God's family that comes through my faith in Jesus Christ.
Holiness is my ______________ of becoming like Christ.
Holiness comes by my ________________ to God's Word.

Notes from My Mentor's Personal Experience

Scripture Memory Chapter Eight

"For our sake he made him to be sin who knew no sin, so that in him we might become the righteousness of God." (II Corinthians 5:21)

Chapter Nine

A LIFE OF PEACE

"Therefore, we are ambassadors for Christ, God making his appeal through us. We implore you on behalf of Christ, be reconciled to God." (II Corinthians 5:20)

The third piece of armor is the Shoes of the preparation of the Gospel of Peace. The Great Commission becomes our mission. The Gospel is the good news that man can have peace with God. This is the first of the offensive weapons.

I was on an airplane and the pilot announced that we were flying at thirty-five thousand feet. I felt prompted to ask the man next to me, "How high did he say we were flying?" He responded, "Thirty-five thousand feet." "Wow!" I said, "Do you think you will ever get any closer to Heaven than this?" He said, "I hope so." I responded, "Would you like to know so, if you could?" He said, "Yes." I shared Christ with him and he accepted Jesus right there in his seat. As it turned out, his mother had been sharing Christ with him and praying for his salvation for many years. What prompted me to say what I did? Was it an angel whispering in my ear or was it the Holy Spirit telling me what to do?

We are to march forward into the world with the gospel of peace. Before we march into battle, we must be prepared. We need to put on the appropriate shoes for the battlefield. We do not put on slippers. We put on heavy combat boots. We cannot win the battle if our feet are cut and bleeding from the debris that is scattered all over the field. With the gospel of peace, we are to free the captives. Satan is holding lost sinners as prisoners and slaves to sin. We have been commissioned by Christ to release them from the enemy. In Second Corinthians, we are told about our responsibility in this area.

> *I march into the world to rescue Satan's captives with the gospel of peace*

> *"All this is from God, who through Christ reconciled us to himself and gave us the ministry of reconciliation; that is, in Christ God was reconciling the world to himself, not counting their trespasses against them, and entrusting to us the message of reconciliation. Therefore, we are ambassadors for Christ, God making his appeal through us. We implore you on behalf of Christ, be reconciled to God."* (II Corinthians 5:18-20)

The Great Commission was given five times in the New Testament by the Lord Jesus:

1. *"And Jesus came and said to them, "All authority in heaven and on earth has been given to me. Go therefore and make disciples of all nations, baptizing them in the name of the Father*

and of the Son and of the Holy Spirit, teaching them to observe all that I have commanded you. And behold, I am with you always, to the end of the age." (Matthew 28:18-20)

2. *"And he said to them, "Go into all the world and proclaim the gospel to the whole creation."* (Mark 16:15)
3. *"And that repentance and forgiveness of sins should be proclaimed in his name to all nations, beginning from Jerusalem." (Luke 24:47)*
4. *"As you sent me into the world, so I have sent them into the world. Jesus said to them again, …Peace be with you. As the Father has sent me, even so I am sending you."* (John 17:18, 20:21)
5. *"But you will receive power when the Holy Spirit has come upon you, and you will be my witnesses in Jerusalem and in all Judea and Samaria, and to the end of the earth."* (Acts 1:8)

Evangelizing the world is my primary mission

Sharing the gospel with the world is the mission of the church. We must preach the gospel to the whole world before Christ returns. It is not our job to Christianize the entire world because not all people will believe. Our responsibility is to share the gospel, which means that all must hear about Christ.

In Romans 10:13, it tells us that, *"For "everyone who calls on the name of the Lord will be saved."* Verse 14 seems to indicate that it may not be that easy. It asks three questions that challenge us to do our part in helping people call on the Lord. *"How then will they call on him in whom they have not believed? And how are they to believe in him of whom they have never heard? And how are they to hear without someone preaching?"*

1. How shall they ask Him to save them unless they believe in Him?

The unsaved cannot call on the Lord to save them until they believe. *"For I delivered to you as of first importance what I also received: that Christ died for our sins in accordance with the Scriptures, that he was buried, that he was raised on the third day in accordance with the Scriptures,"* (I Corinthians 15:3-4)

> *"Whoever believes in him is not condemned, but whoever does not believe is condemned already, because he has not believed in the name of the only Son of God. Whoever believes in the Son has eternal life; whoever does not obey the Son shall not see life, but the wrath of God remains on him."* (John 3:18, 36)

2. How can they believe in Him if they have never heard about Him?

The unsaved cannot believe in Christ until they hear the Gospel of salvation. In the book of Acts, we find people who had to hear to believe. Following, I have included four wonderful Biblical stories and an experience of my own that show how the Holy Spirit prepares both the one sharing Christ and the one receiving the message. It reminds us that

The Holy Spirit prepares and convicts people of their need for Christ

it is the Holy Spirit's job to prepare and convict a person of their need for Christ. Our job is just to share. In these stories, you will see how clearly the Holy Spirit does His work.

The Eunuch had to hear to believe:

> *"Now an angel of the Lord said to Philip, "Rise and go toward the south to the road that goes down from Jerusalem to Gaza." This is a desert place. And he rose and went. And there was an Ethiopian, a eunuch, a court official of Candace, queen of the Ethiopians, who was in charge of all her treasure. He had come to Jerusalem to worship and was returning, seated in his chariot, and he was reading the prophet Isaiah. And the Spirit said to Philip, "Go over and join this chariot." So Philip ran to him and heard him reading Isaiah the prophet and asked, "Do you understand what you are reading?" And he said, "How can I, unless someone guides me?" And he invited Philip to come up and sit with him. Now the passage of the Scripture that he was reading was this: Like a sheep he was led to the slaughter and like a lamb before its shearer is silent, so he opens not his mouth. In his humiliation justice was denied him. Who can describe his generation? For his life is taken away from the earth."*
>
> *And the eunuch said to Philip, "About whom, I ask you, does the prophet say this, about himself or about someone else?" Then*

> *Philip opened his mouth, and beginning with this Scripture he told him the good news about Jesus. And as they were going along the road they came to some water, and the eunuch said, "See, here is water! What prevents me from being baptized? And Philip said, "If you believe with all your heart, you may." And he replied, "I believe that Jesus Christ is the Son of God."* (Acts 8:26-37)

Paul had to hear to believe:

> *"But Saul, still breathing threats and murder against the disciples of the Lord, went to the high priest and asked him for letters to the synagogues at Damascus, so that if he found any belonging to the Way, men or women, he might bring them bound to Jerusalem. Now as he went on his way, he approached Damascus, and suddenly a light from heaven shone around him. And falling to the ground he heard a voice saying to him, "Saul, Saul, why are you persecuting me?" And he said, "Who are you, Lord?" And he said, "I am Jesus, whom you are persecuting. But rise and enter the city, and you will be told what you are to do." The men who were traveling with him stood speechless, hearing the voice but seeing no one. Saul rose from the ground, and although his eyes were opened, he saw nothing. So they led him by the hand and brought him into Damascus. And for three*

days he was without sight, and neither ate nor drank.

Now there was a disciple at Damascus named Ananias. The Lord said to him in a vision, "Ananias." And he said, "Here I am, Lord." And the Lord said to him, "Rise and go to the street called Straight, and at the house of Judas look for a man of Tarsus named Saul, for behold, he is praying, and he has seen in a vision a man named Ananias come in and lay his hands on him so that he might regain his sight." But Ananias answered, "Lord, I have heard from many about this man, how much evil he has done to your saints at Jerusalem. And here he has authority from the chief priests to bind all who call on your name." But the Lord said to him, "Go, for he is a chosen instrument of mine to carry my name before the Gentiles and kings and the children of Israel. For I will show him how much he must suffer for the sake of my name." So Ananias departed and entered the house. And laying his hands on him he said, "Brother Saul, the Lord Jesus who appeared to you on the road by which you came has sent me so that you may regain your sight and be filled with the Holy Spirit." And immediately something like scales fell from his eyes, and he regained his sight. Then he rose and was baptized;" (Acts 9:1-18)

Cornelius had to hear to believe:

> *"At Caesarea there was a man named Cornelius, a centurion of what was known as the Italian Cohort, a devout man who feared God with all his household, gave alms generously to the people, and prayed continually to God. About the ninth hour of the day he saw clearly in a vision an angel of God come in and say to him, "Cornelius." And he stared at him in terror and said, "What is it, Lord?" And he said to him, "Your prayers and your alms have ascended as a memorial before God. And now send men to Joppa and bring one Simon who is called Peter. He is lodging with one Simon, a tanner, whose house is by the sea." When the angel who spoke to him had departed, he called two of his servants and a devout soldier from among those who attended him, and having related everything to them, he sent them to Joppa.*
>
> *The next day, as they were on their journey and approaching the city, Peter went up on the housetop about the sixth hour to pray. And he became hungry and wanted something to eat, but while they were preparing it, he fell into a trance and saw the heavens opened and something like a great sheet descending, being let down by its four corners upon the earth. In it were all kinds of animals and reptiles and birds of the air. And there came a voice to him: "Rise, Peter;*

kill and eat." But Peter said, "By no means, Lord; for I have never eaten anything that is common or unclean." And the voice came to him again a second time, "What God has made clean, do not call common." This happened three times, and the thing was taken up at once to heaven.

Now while Peter was inwardly perplexed as to what the vision that he had seen might mean, behold, the men who were sent by Cornelius, having made inquiry for Simon's house, stood at the gate and called out to ask whether Simon who was called Peter was lodging there. And while Peter was pondering the vision, the Spirit said to him, "Behold, three men are looking for you. Rise and go down and accompany them without hesitation, for I have sent them." And Peter went down to the men and said, "I am the one you are looking for. What is the reason for your coming?" 22 *And they said, "Cornelius, a centurion, an upright and God-fearing man, who is well spoken of by the whole Jewish nation, was directed by a holy angel to send for you to come to his house and to hear what you have to say." So he invited them in to be his guests.*

The next day he rose and went away with them, and some of the brothers from Joppa accompanied him. And on the following day they entered Caesarea. Cornelius was expecting them and had called together his relatives and close friends. When Peter entered, Cornelius met him and fell down at his feet and worshiped him. But Peter lifted him up, saying, "Stand up; I too am a man." And as he talked with him, he went in and found many persons gathered. And he said to them, "You yourselves know how unlawful it is for a Jew to associate with or to visit anyone of another nation, but God has shown me that I should not call any person common or unclean. So when I was sent for, I came without objection. I ask then why you sent for me."

And Cornelius said, "Four days ago, about this hour, I was praying in my house at the ninth hour, and behold, a man stood before me in bright clothing and said, 'Cornelius, your prayer has been heard and your alms have been remembered before God. Send therefore to Joppa and ask for Simon who is called Peter. He is lodging in the house of Simon, a tanner, by the sea.' So I sent for you at once, and you have been kind enough to come. Now therefore we are all here in the presence of God to hear all that you have been commanded by the Lord."

So Peter opened his mouth and said: "Truly I understand that God shows no partiality, but in every nation anyone who fears him and does what is right is acceptable to him. As for the word that he sent to Israel, preaching good news of peace through Jesus

Christ (he is Lord of all), you yourselves know what happened throughout all Judea, beginning from Galilee after the baptism that John proclaimed: how God anointed Jesus of Nazareth with the Holy Spirit and with power. He went about doing good and healing all who were oppressed by the devil, for God was with him. And we are witnesses of all that he did both in the country of the Jews and in Jerusalem. They put him to death by hanging him on a tree, but God raised him on the third day and made him to appear, not to all the people but to us who had been chosen by God as witnesses, who ate and drank with him after he rose from the dead. And he commanded us to preach to the people and to testify that he is the one appointed by God to be judge of the living and the dead. To him all the prophets bear witness that everyone who believes in him receives forgiveness of sins through his name."

While Peter was still saying these things, the Holy Spirit fell on all who heard the word. And the believers from among the circumcised who had come with Peter were amazed, because the gift of the Holy Spirit was poured out even on the Gentiles. For they were hearing them speaking in tongues and extolling God. Then Peter declared, "Can anyone withhold water for baptizing these people, who have received the Holy Spirit just as we have?" And he commanded

> *them to be baptized in the name of Jesus Christ. Then they asked him to remain for some days. (Acts 10:1-48)*

The Philippians jailer had to hear to believe:

> *"About midnight Paul and Silas were praying and singing hymns to God, and the prisoners were listening to them, and suddenly there was a great earthquake, so that the foundations of the prison were shaken. And immediately all the doors were opened, and everyone's bonds were unfastened. When the jailer woke and saw that the prison doors were open, he drew his sword and was about to kill himself, supposing that the prisoners had escaped. But Paul cried with a loud voice, "Do not harm yourself, for we are all here." And the jailer called for lights and rushed in, and trembling with fear he fell down before Paul and Silas. Then he brought them out and said, "Sirs, what must I do to be saved?" And they said, "Believe in the Lord Jesus, and you will be saved, you and your household." And they spoke the word of the Lord to him and to all who were in his house. And he took them the same hour of the night and washed their wounds; and he was baptized at once, he and all his family. Then he brought them up into his house and set food before them. And he rejoiced along with his entire household that he had believed in God." (Acts 16:25-34)*

Did you notice how angels worked to prepare both the person receiving the message and the person delivering it? The Holy Spirit also got directly involved in leading individuals to those He had already prepared. In one case, God used an earthquake to provide the right opportunity for a witness to be given. He also used the Word of God and the testimony of other believers. God is not limited in His resources to help us proclaim the gospel of peace when we are willing and prepared to share Christ.

Angels prepare both the person receiving the message and the person delivering it

A personal experience where God used my car to witness:

In 1979, Tyndale House Publishers, Inc. published my life story entitled, "The Down Way Up, The Roy Comstock Story," written by Carole Gift Page. In it, she tells a story about an experience I had where God used my 1956 Oldsmobile to assist in winning eleven people to Christ.

> In early 1962, buoyed by a new zeal to serve the Lord, Roy joined a dozen young men from Lakewood who were organizing a gospel team. Shortly after joining the team, an incident once again raised the question for Roy: Should he enter the ministry? One Sunday evening, the team drove down to San Diego to speak in a small Baptist church on Coronado Island. They received a tremendous response, with a number of people finding Christ as Savior.

After the service, the team's three-car caravan pushed through murky fog toward the ferry that would take them off the island. Suddenly, as they neared the ferry, Roy's 1956 Oldsmobile stopped dead. All the young men piled out of their cars and swarmed around Roy's stalled vehicle. "I can't figure out what's wrong," he told them. "The engine's absolutely dead."

A little red-headed fellow spoke up, "Well, Praise the Lord. He must want us to do something here." Someone else said, "Hey, there's a place to eat over there. Let's go in and maybe the car will start when we come back." Everyone agreed. They were all starved! Entering the dimly lit restaurant, they realized it was also a bar. "Well, this is the only place open and we're stuck here," said Roy, "Might as well make the best of it." When the hostess came to seat them, Roy asked for a table away from the bar. She led them to a small private room where they were all able to sit at one table. While they waited for their food, they could hear the baritone singer in the next room belting out a popular song.

"Hey, wouldn't it be neat if we could sing our kind of music here," said one of the guys. "Why can't we?" asked someone else. A third youth responded, "Okay, I'll get my trombone and music." "And I'll get my trumpet," added a fourth fellow. Minutes later, the team's quartet stood beside their table singing gospel songs. It didn't take long for the manager, a squat little Jewish lady, to bustle in and snap angrily, "You can't do that in here!" One of the team members rose to his full seven feet and placed his hand lightly on her shoulder. "Would you please come over here and let me talk to you about this?" he asked. He took her over to one corner and witnessed briefly about Christ. After that she let them sing.

Shortly, the baritone from the other room came in and stood behind the quartet looking at the music. "I don't know these words," he said, "But let me sing with you guys. You sound pretty good." They sang together for a while then one of the team members began talking to the vocalist about Jesus. He led him to the Lord right there at the table.

Meanwhile Roy and Ron, the manager of the gospel team, sat chatting at the other end of the table. When the waiter came over to refill their water glasses, they both spoke at once: "Whoever drinks of this water shall thirst again; but whoever drinks of the water that I shall give him shall never thirst." The waiter looked puzzled. "What are you guys talking about?" Roy and Ron exchanged sly grins. Here was their cue. They shared their testimony. Moments later, the man knelt between them at the table and asked Christ into his life. Before long, other customers gathered curiously around the gospel team, listening to their music and asking questions about their faith. Before the team left the restaurant that night, nine people prayed to receive Christ as Savior.

When Roy returned to his car, he fully expected it to start. It didn't. He looked over at Ron and sighed, "Now what? Any ideas how we can get off this island?" One of the guys spoke up from the back seat. "Well, we're close to the ferry. You see those two attendants in the booth over there? Maybe that's why we're still here." "Let's find out," said Ron, opening the car door. He and the other team member went over and talked with the two men. When they returned a little later, Ron was grinning jubilantly. "They both accepted Christ!" he exclaimed. Amid cheers and praises, Roy tried the ignition again. The engine turned over and purred smoothly.

God is not limited in His resources to help us proclaim the gospel

3. How can they hear about Him unless someone tells them?

They cannot hear unless someone tells them. Three thousand were saved at Pentecost because of one hundred twenty witnesses. *"In those days Peter stood up among the brothers (the company of persons was in all about 120) and said, ...So those who received his word were baptized, and there were added that day about three thousand souls."* (Act 1:15, 2:41)

We have already read about the eunuch that believed because Philip witnessed. Paul believed because Jesus the God-man, and Ananias witnessed. We also see in Acts chapter seven, where Stephen witnessed to Paul.

> *"Now when they heard these things they were enraged, and they ground their teeth at him. But he, full of the Holy Spirit, gazed into heaven and saw the glory of God, and Jesus standing at the right hand of God. And he said, "Behold, I see the heavens opened, and the Son of Man standing at the right hand of God." But they cried out with a loud voice and stopped their ears and rushed together at him. Then they cast him out of the city and stoned him. And the witnesses laid down their garments at the feet of a young man named Saul. And as they were stoning Stephen, he called out, "Lord Jesus, receive my spirit." And falling to his knees he cried out with a loud voice, "Lord, do not hold this sin against them." And when he had said this, he fell asleep." (Acts 7:54-60)*

We also read that Cornelius and his household were saved because Peter witnessed. The Philippians jailer was saved because Paul and Silas witnessed. And you and I were saved because someone witnessed to us. Think about how you came to know about Jesus Christ and how you discovered your need for salvation. Who were the people most responsible for you accepting Christ?

A witness is one who simply tells what he saw or experienced. Be prepared to tell others how you came to Christ and what He has meant in your life. Write your testimony out on paper to make it clear. Tell about your life before you accepted Christ, how you came to Christ, and what changes have taken place since you received Him.

GOD USES OUR TESTIMONY

Jesus Christ gave us the commission to tell the whole world about His wonderful plan of salvation. We are to carry the message of the Gospel to every person He brings into our lives (center of influence). God uses our testimony of how we came to Christ to convince others of their need for Him. God also uses it to defeat Satan. *"And they have conquered him by the blood of the Lamb and by the word of their testimony, for they loved not their lives even unto death."* (Revelation 12:11)

A witness is one who simply tells what he has seen or experienced

According to the Word of God, the unsaved cannot be saved without a witness. They must have a witness to hear, they must hear to believe, they must believe to call, and they must call to be saved. But they cannot call until they believe, they cannot believe until they hear, and they cannot hear without a witness, *"So faith comes from hearing, and hearing through the word of Christ."* (Romans 10:17). We are not born with saving faith; it comes only when we hear the Gospel. Therefore, it is of utmost importance that every born again child of God obeys the Great Commission to evangelize.

While I was writing this book in prison, the only study Bible I had available was the Open Bible. Therefore, most of the outline of this chapter is an adaptation of the reference notes on the bottom of pages 1064 and 1065. Used by permission.

Chapter Nine

A LIFE OF PEACE

Questions for home study and group discussion

What questions are asked in Romans 10:14?

How did Philip know to witness to the eunuch?
Acts 8:26-37

How did Ananias know that he was to witness to Paul?
Acts 9:10-18

How did Cornelius know to send for Peter, and how did Peter know how to respond? Acts 10:1-48

What did Paul and Silas do when the Philippians jailer asked, "Sirs, what must I do to be saved?" Acts 16:25-34

Notes from My Mentor's Experiences

ScriptureMemory Chapter Nine

"Therefore, we are ambassadors for Christ, God making his appeal through us. We implore you on behalf of Christ, be reconciled to God." (II Corinthians 5:20)

CHAPTER TEN

A LIFE OF FAITH

"Now faith is the assurance of things hoped for, the conviction of things not seen." (Hebrews 11:1)

We will have a life of faith by putting on this fourth piece of armor called the Shield of Faith. *"In all circumstances take up the shield of faith, with which you can extinguish all the flaming darts of the evil one;"* (Ephesians 6:16) Paul says that the proper use of the Shield of Faith assures us that we will stop every attempt of Satan to attack us. Satan cannot overcome true faith. What is faith? *"Now faith is the assurance of things hoped for, the conviction of things not seen." (Hebrews 11:1)* In the New King James it says; "*Now, faith is the substance of things hoped for, the evidence of things not seen.*" In the Living Bible it says, "*What is faith? It is the confident assurance that something we want is going to happen. It is the certainty that what we hope for is waiting for us, even though we cannot see it up ahead.*"

Faith is more than belief. Belief can be an intellectual consent, but faith is the action we take as a result of what we believe. To better understand the difference between belief and faith, consider this story about a tightrope walker over Niagara Falls.

The circus had come to town, and in order to draw a crowd, one of the tightrope walkers had strung a high wire from one side of the falls to the other. It spanned the dangerous water below. As the falls pounded against the rocks below, the tightrope walker walked back and forth several times. Finally, he started riding a bike across and back again. The crowd began to grow, astonished at this daring. He stopped at the edge of the crowd and asked, "How many of you believe I can ride my bike over to the other side of the falls on that rope?" The crowd cheered. They all shouted, "We believe you can!" He asked, "How many of you believe I can carry another person on the bike with me to the other side?" The crowd again cheered and agreed that he could. So he turned to a man at the edge of the crowd. "Do you believe that I can take a person on this bike with me to the other side?" "Oh Yes!" he exclaimed. So the tightrope walker challenged him to get on. But the man took off like a flash into the crowd. The man professed that he believed, but he did not put his belief into action. Faith is belief in action.

Faith is the action I take as a result of what I believe

So you say that you believe in Christ? But the question is, "Have you put your knowledge and belief into action?" Have you put your complete trust in Him? Or is your profession like the man in the crowd? You must be willing to get on the bike! You must, by an act of your will, place yourself in Christ's care and know in your heart that He will do what He promises. *"But to all who did receive him, who believed in his name, he gave the right to become children of God,"* (John 1:12) You can believe all you want about Christ, but until you receive Him into your life, you have not yet exercised saving faith.

If you were caught in a building fire and had to leap out into the arms of the firemen to safety but, instead, you stood in the burning room, all the belief and knowledge couldn't save you. Saving faith is faith that acts on what you believe. This is not only true regarding our salvation, but it is also true in our exercise of faith for God's daily provision. We claim to believe that God will provide our every need, but we continue to worry in fear that our needs may not be met. That is not the kind of faith that is talked about in Hebrews 11:1 above. When we do this, we have little faith.

PETER DEMONSTRATED LITTLE FAITH

In Matthew, one of the most notable stories of the Apostle Peter took place on the sea just after Jesus had ministered to a large crowd. Telling His disciples to go ahead of Him to the other side of the sea, Jesus went off to pray. Late in the evening, His disciples were in a boat somewhere in the middle of the sea when they saw Jesus from a distance.

> *"Immediately he made the disciples get into the boat and go before him to the other side, while he dismissed the crowds. And after he had dismissed the crowds, he went up on the mountain by himself to pray. When evening came, he was there alone, but the boat by this time was a long way from the land, beaten by the waves, for the wind was against them. And in the fourth watch of the night he came to them, walking on the sea. But when the disciples saw him walking on the sea, they were terrified, and said, "It is a ghost!" and they cried out in fear.*

> *But immediately Jesus spoke to them, saying, "Take heart; it is I. Do not be afraid."*
>
> *And Peter answered him, "Lord, if it is you, command me to come to you on the water." He said, "Come." So Peter got out of the boat and walked on the water and came to Jesus. But when he saw the wind, he was afraid, and beginning to sink he cried out, "Lord, save me." Jesus immediately reached out his hand and took hold of him, saying to him, "O you of little faith, why did you doubt?" And when they got into the boat, the wind ceased. And those in the boat worshiped him, saying, "Truly you are the Son of God."* (Matthew 14:22-33)

You can imagine their fright and awe! When Jesus drew near to their boat, Peter looked out and said, "Lord if you command me to come out to you on the water, I will." Jesus said, "Come." At first, Peter's belief was strong, so he acted on his conviction and stepped out onto the water. Well, almost as soon as he began to accomplish the impossible and walk on the water, he looked around to what was, in his mind, unfathomable and fear gripped him. Immediately, Peter began to sink.

Let's examine Peter's faith. We can benefit from a close look at Peter's little faith. Peter was with the disciples on their boat in the midst of a tremendous storm. The disciples saw what appeared to be a ghost and it frightened them. But Jesus spoke and said, "Don't be troubled, it is me." Peter said, "Lord, if it's really you, then let me walk out on the water to meet you." Jesus said, "Come."

Peter acted

He acted by faith and walked on water. He believed and then acted by faith on what he believed. It would be easy for us to exclaim, "Wow!" That sounds like a lot of faith to me. After all, the other disciples didn't even attempt to step out onto the water. How can we say that Peter had little faith? Jesus said, "O thou of little faith, wherefore didst thou doubt?" His faith was little compared to the faith that God desires for His children to exercise.

Peter doubted his decision

He doubted. For a moment, he lost sight of Jesus. He probably looked back at the boat and realized that he was in an impossible situation. He may have said, "What am I doing? Man can't walk on water, how stupid of me to think I could just walk out here like this."

Peter feared destruction

He feared destruction. Doubt always creates fear. He lost sight of the thing he hoped for. Faith is the substance of things hoped for. Peter hoped to walk over to Jesus on the water. He acted by faith on what he believed would happen. This is an example of how Satan works. He knows that if he can get our eyes off Jesus and onto the circumstances in our life, then we will begin to doubt and lose hope.

Peter was discouraged and felt defeated

He failed. The problem wasn't what he believed, or for that matter, his faith in what he believed. He started out believing. The problem was the time it took him between acting on his faith and the manifestation or completion of the thing he hoped to accomplish. He hoped to walk to Jesus and back to the boat again. Peter had said, *"Lord, if it be thou, bid me come unto thee on the water."* One of Satan's greatest tools against the believer is discouragement. If he can discourage us, he knows that he has a good chance of defeating us.

Faith is the evidence of things not seen, the certainty that what we hoped for is up ahead, even though we can't see it. Perhaps, in the midst of the storm, Peter lost sight of Jesus. Jesus may have been referring to Peter's little faith because Peter only had faith as long as he could see where he was going. Sometimes we allow the storms in our lives to overwhelm us to the point where we also lose faith and focus our eyes upon our problems instead of putting faith in Jesus, the master of the ship. Trusting in Him to guide us through even the most violent of storms, we find refuge in the safe harbor of His bosom.

> *Faith is the confident assurance that something I believe in will happen even though I cannot see it*

The area most of us have problems with is the sustaining hope that carries us through the storm safely to our destination. However, hope standing alone has no substance. Hope is a dream. Substance means that which is material. What faith does is give hope substance. Hope is the goal. The goal has no substance. Your faith gives your goal substance until it materializes or manifests itself.

> *My faith gives my goals substance until they materialize or manifest themselves*

Recently, a friend of mine told me about a television documentary he'd seen lately of an unusual woman who lives along the Alaskan Coast. A number of years ago, this amazing woman began to swim in the freezing Arctic Ocean, acting on her belief she could do it. Because of the fatal nature of hypothermia, a normal person would quickly succumb to the death grip of the extremely cold waters. But after many years of acting on her belief that it was possible, she recently swam for just over an hour in the frigid waters. Her faith defied what is considered impossible.

Peter turned back to Jesus

He prayed, "Lord, save me." And immediately, Jesus stretched forth his hand and caught him. Once more, Peter made contact with Jesus by faith. What Peter hoped for was to walk over to Jesus on the water and back to the boat. He lost sight of his objective because he became frightened by the circumstances around him. But when he got his eyes off the circumstances and back on Jesus, he did the right thing; he asked for Jesus' help. He put himself completely under Jesus' control. He realized that there was nothing that he could do for himself. He had to trust Jesus to guide him through the storm.

We have to get our eyes off the circumstances around us and back on Jesus. His Word promises us that, *"And my God will supply every need of yours according to his riches in glory in Christ Jesus."* (Philippians 4:19) How do we keep our hope in the middle of a storm? How do we keep from getting discouraged? How do we keep from giving up and sinking? We must keep our faith in God's promises in front of us.

We believe in Jesus Christ for our salvation, but we must also know the Word of God and the promises God gives to all of His children. The Word says, "*And we know that for those who love God all things work together for good, for those who are called according to his purpose.*" (Romans 8:28) This verse does not say that everything that comes into our lives is good. It doesn't say that God is the only source of

God uses every circumstance in my life for good

things coming into our lives. It does promise, however, that God will use every circumstance in our life for good.

Peter becomes victorious

Again, Peter succeeded by walking on the water with Jesus. What was the difference? The storm was still raging about Peter. Matthew 14:32 says, "*And when they came into the ship, the wind ceased.*" The storm didn't stop until after Peter was back in the boat.

The difference was that Peter refocused his attention on his objective. Instead of dwelling on his problems, he turned to the source of his faith, Jesus Christ. Paul tells us in Romans that, *"For by the grace given to me I say to everyone among you not to think of himself more highly than he ought to think, but to think with sober judgment, each according to the measure of faith that God has assigned."* (Romans 12:3) He also said, *"So then faith cometh by hearing, and hearing by the Word of God."* (Romans 10:17) Peter spent time with Jesus Christ who Himself is the Word. *"In the beginning was the Word, and the Word was with God, and the Word was God. … And the Word became flesh and dwelt among us, and we have seen his glory, glory as of the only Son from the Father, full of grace and truth."* (John 1:1, 14) Peter's faith came from hearing Jesus, the Word, speak and teach for three years. Jesus was Peter's source of faith.

God's Word is like the instrument panel on an airplane. You have to fly by the instruments instead of visually. Have you ever been in an airplane on a stormy night? Visibility is almost zero. The pilot must rely on his instruments to fly and land the plane. The pilot must also understand the instruments and know how to use them. He must believe they work before he can put his faith in them. He will be in serious trouble if he has little faith and doubts their reliability to guide the plane to its destination.

Commercial pilots often fly in adverse weather conditions. One night, a flight that I was on going into Hong Kong was completely shrouded in dense fog and clouds. In order to get the plane and passengers safely to the airport, the pilot had to rely completely on his instruments. They tell him what to do. He must also talk to the tower for special insight concerning his situation. He needs to know whether other pilots are having the same problem and how they are handling it. He must act by faith on what he believes. He looks out the window; he can't see anything but darkness. As his instruments guide him closer to the ground, it looks even worse. All he can see are clouds. Even flying with zero visibility, he brings the plane right down onto the runway. He carefully follows an invisible radio beam, a cluster of meters, and variety of indicator lights that display altitude, horizon, and direction. The pilot who doesn't rely on what he sees, but on what he believes his instruments tell him, will land his plane on the runway every time.

God's Words are my instruments and I have learned to trust my instruments

God's words are our instruments and we must learn to trust our instruments. If we can see where we are going and how we are going to get there, we don't need faith, because faith is the evidence of things not seen. We must believe God's Word and act on it by faith. God says that He will supply all of our needs according to His riches in glory in Christ Jesus. Do we believe that? In the midst of difficult circumstances, can we believe that? Even though we can't see a way out of our problems, do we believe that God will supply our need?

I walk by faith, not by sight

If we could see the way out ourselves, it would require no faith. If we are going to walk by faith and not by sight (II Corinthians 5:7), then we must put our faith in "that which is not seen." We have to let God's Word guide us.

PETER DID NOT LET TEMPORARY FAILURE DESTROY HIM

Peter put his trust back in the right thing: Jesus Christ and His Word. Peter was failing, he was sinking, but he didn't drown. Even though he temporarily failed, he didn't stop trying. He got his eyes off the circumstances and back on what he hoped for. He then succeeded in finishing what he had believed was possible. Even though in the natural, it appeared to be impossible. Peter experienced success because he didn't let temporary failure determine his future. He did what Paul said he did. Paul said, *"Brothers, I do not consider that I have made it my own. But one thing I do: forgetting what lies behind and straining forward to what lies ahead, I press on toward the goal for the prize of the upward call of God in Christ Jesus."* (Philippians 3:13-14) Paul admits that he has not arrived, but he refuses to dwell on his past. Paul says that he is forgetting the past and putting all his energies toward the accomplishment of his future goals.

God forgave me of my mistakes and failures, not just my sins

We must learn to forget our past. If we continue to dwell on the past, Satan will use those memories of failure to keep us from trying to do what God wants us to do now and in the future. So you've failed miserably. So what? God doesn't care. Forget it. God will forgive you - just ask Him. *"If we confess our sins, he is faithful and just to forgive us our sins and to cleanse us from all unrighteousness."* (I John 1:9) God will also forgive you of your mistakes and failures, not just your sins. We feel so useless because we keep failing over and over. God knows that, yet He loves us anyway. You must also learn to forgive yourself. If God, in all His holiness, can look at you, in all your sinfulness, and accept you just like you are and call you His child, why not forgive yourself? Here is a statement you can repeat to yourself daily, "I walk by faith not by sight. I keep my faith in Jesus Christ. I don't let circumstances and failures defeat me. I learn from them and then put them behind me and press forward to my goal, to daily conform to the image of Christ."

"In all circumstances take up the shield of faith, with which you can extinguish all the flaming darts of the evil one: (Ephesians 6:16) Putting on this piece of armor is truly walking by faith, not by sight. Satan cannot win in his attacks against a person who knows how to use the Shield of Faith.

Chapter Ten

A LIFE OF FAITH

Questions for home study and group discussion

How do you define faith?
Hebrews 11:1

What part do actions play in your faith?
James 2:18

What did you learn from Peter's little faith?
Matthew 14:22-33

Where does faith come from?
Romans 10:17, 12:3b

What are some of the ways we can practice our faith?
II Corinthians 5:7, Philippians 3:12-14, I John 1:9

Notes from My Mentor's Personal Experiences

Scripture Memory Chapter Ten

"Now faith is the assurance of things hoped for, the conviction of things not seen." (Hebrews 11:1)

CHAPTER ELEVEN

A LIFE OF ASSURANCE

> *"And this is the testimony that God gave us eternal life, and this life is in his Son. Whoever has the Son has life; whoever does not have the Son of God does not have life. I write these things to you who believe in the name of the Son of God that you may know that you have eternal life."* (I John 5:11-13)

Chapter eleven will cover both the fifth and sixth piece of armor. The fifth piece of armor is the Helmet of Salvation. We have already talked about salvation. The most important thing is that we know without any doubt that we are saved. If you have any questions about whether or not you are going to Heaven, go back to Characteristic One and reread it until you are sure that you have Christ as your personal Savior.

When you are sure that you have Christ as your Savior, Satan can't get into your head and try to lead you down the road into false doctrine. The Helmet of Salvation protects you from confu-

I know Jesus Christ as my personal Savior and Lord

sion concerning your relationship and position with Jesus Christ.

"For by grace you have been saved through faith. And this is not your own doing; it is the gift of God, not a result of works, so that no one may boast." (Ephesians 2:8-9) If you could live a good enough life to meet God's holy standard, then Christ wasted His life here on earth by dying on the cross. Eternal life is a free gift, you receive it instantly the moment that you pray and invite Christ into your heart. In that moment, your eternal destiny changes from hell to Heaven. The matter is settled for all eternity. Nothing can separate you from the love of Christ.

> *I am saved by grace through my faith and not by my works; it is a gift of God*

> *"What then shall we say to these things? If God is for us, who can be against us? He who did not spare his own Son but gave him up for us all, how will he not also with him graciously give us all things? Who shall bring any charge against God's elect? It is God who justifies. Who is to condemn? Christ Jesus is the one who died—more than that, who was raised—who is at the right hand of God, who indeed is interceding for us. Who shall separate us from the love of Christ? Shall tribulation, or distress, or persecution, or famine, or nakedness, or danger, or sword? As it is written,*
>
> > *"For your sake we are being killed all the day long; we are regarded as sheep to be slaughtered."*

"No, in all these things we are more than conquerors through him who loved us. For I am sure that neither death nor life, nor angels nor rulers, nor things present nor things to come, nor powers, nor height nor depth, nor anything else in all creation, will be able to separate us from the love of God in Christ Jesus our Lord." (Romans 8:31-39)

A LIFE OF HIS WORD

"For the word of God is living and active, sharper than any two-edged sword, piercing to the division of soul and of spirit, of joints and of marrow, and discerning the thoughts and intentions of the heart." (Hebrews 4:12)

The sixth piece of armor is the Sword of the Spirit, which is the Word of God. While talking about faith, we discussed the idea of walking by faith, not by sight. This means walking in the Word of God. The illustration about the airplane pilot putting his faith in his instruments was to illustrate that we must put our faith in God's Word. The object of the Christian's faith is Jesus Christ, and we know Him through the Word of God. The Word determines what we believe. When we act by faith, we are acting on what we believe the Word of God teaches.

The triune God speaks to me through His Word

The Word of God: Oh, what a powerful statement. These are the words of God the Father, God the Son, and God the Holy Spirit. The triune God speaks to you and me through His Word. This is not a book like any other book that just gives instructions or information. It is the voice of God Almighty speaking to our hearts. The one who created everything and who holds it all together with His own power is speaking to us through the Bible. Yet, we so often leave it sitting around unattended as if it were just an ordinary book. We must take a close look at Hebrews 4:12 in order to begin to understand the power of God's Word in our lives. The Amplified Bible states it as follows:

> *"For the Word of God speaks and is alive and full of power [making it active, operative, energizing, and effective]; it is sharper than any two-edged sword, penetrating to the dividing line of the breath of life (soul) and [the immortal] spirit, and of joints and marrow [of the deepest parts of our nature], exposing and sifting and analyzing and judging the very thoughts and purposes of the heart."* (Hebrews 4:12 Amplified)

There are fourteen descriptive words in this verse that begin to explain the Word of God.

For the Word of God:

1.	Speaks	and is
2.	Alive	
3.	Powerful	making it
4.	Active	
5.	Operative	
6.	Energizing	
7.	Effective	it is
8.	Sharper	than any two-edged sword
9.	Penetrating	to the

10. Dividing — line of the breath of life (soul) and (the immortal) spirit, and the joints and marrow (of the deepest parts of our nature)
11. Exposing
12. Sifting
13. Analyzing
14. Judging — (discerning) the very thoughts and purposes (intents) of the heart.

It is important for us to remember that we will always act out in life what we really believe. In order for us to believe in God's Word, we must read and study His Word. We must develop a hunger and a thirst for God's Word in our lives making it active and a real part of our daily living. Our values come from the thoughts and intents of our heart. Hebrews says that the Word of God discerns those thoughts and intents. The Word will also determine them if we allow it to saturate us.

The Psalmist said, "How can a young man keep his way pure? By guarding it according to your word; I have stored up your word in my heart that I might not sin against you." (Psalm 119:9, 11) The Christian's purpose is to conform to the image of Christ. The only way we can do this is by spending time daily in God's Word. It is God's Word that describes Christ's person and life. Without His Word, we have no idea who Christ is or what He taught. We can only accomplish our purpose by daily exposure to Christ through His Word.

As we give complete and daily control of our life to the Holy Spirit, He uses the Bible like a sword against Satan. The sword is an offensive weapon. We are able to attack Satan with the Word. Paul has already explained to us in the book of Ephesians, that this weapon doesn't really belong to us. It is the Sword of the Spirit. When we yield to His control, the

Holy Spirit brings the Word to our remembrance when we need it. He helps us fight the good fight in faith.

The Holy Spirit brings the Word to my remembrance when I need it

We must have God's Word hidden in our heart. It must be there before He can bring it to our remembrance. When we want to use it against Satan, it has to already be in our heart. At the time of the attack, it is too late to decide whether or not we know the Word. We need to have it hidden in our hearts well before the battle starts.

OUR VALUES START WITH OUR THOUGHTS

Our values begin with our thoughts. After we repeat our thoughts over and over, we gradually begin to believe them. As soon as we believe them, they become our values. After they become our values they become our character. Eventually, we begin acting out these characteristics through our behavior. In other words, our actions are a direct reflection of what we allow ourselves to think about over and over. The writer of the Proverbs says, *"for as he calculates in his soul, so is he"* (Proverbs 23:7) The King James says, "*As a man thinketh in his heart, so is he.*" He is telling us that what we dwell on deep within our heart is what we become.

That is why it is so important for us to spend time in God's Word. If we are to become like Christ, we must dwell on His Word and His thoughts. Paul tells us in Philippians, *"Finally, brothers, whatever is true, whatever is honorable, whatever is just, whatever is pure, whatever is lovely, whatever is commendable, if there is any excellence, if there is anything worthy of praise, think about these things." (Philippians 4:8)*

God has given us the right and responsibility to choose what we will think about. You can think about the things of the world or you can think about the things of God, but you cannot know the things of God without studying His Word. God commands us to, *"Do your best to present yourself to God as one approved, a worker who has no need to be ashamed, rightly handling the word of truth."* (II Timothy 2:15) It is not enough to simply read God's Word. In order to be able to understand it completely, apply it to our daily living, we must study it and meditate on it. We must know its contents and meaning thoroughly to be able to properly apply it to all of life's situations.

Paul says, *"Do not be conformed to this world, but be transformed by the renewal of your mind, that by testing you may discern what is the will of God, what is good and acceptable and perfect."* (Romans 12:2) If we spend the majority of our time dwelling on the thoughts of this world, we will think like this world. If we spend time studying God's Word instead of conforming to the world, we will be transformed by the Word of God. God's thoughts will become our thoughts and His values become our values. It all starts with what we think about and hide deep in our hearts. Once we have hidden God's Word in our hearts, we can resist Satan. The Psalmist said, *"I have stored up your word in my heart that I might not sin against you."* (Psalm 119:11)

I am transformed by the renewing of my mind through God's Word

Jesus Christ proved this truth when Satan tempted him. In Matthew, chapter four, we read this account:

> *"Then Jesus was led up by the Spirit into the wilderness to be tempted by the devil. And after fasting forty days and forty nights, he was hungry. And the tempter came and said to him, "If you are the Son of God, command these stones to become loaves of*

bread." But he answered, "It is written, "'Man shall not live by bread alone, but by every word that comes from the mouth of God.'"

"Then the devil took him to the holy city and set him on the pinnacle of the temple and said to him, 'If you are the Son of God, throw yourself down, for it is written, He will command his angels concerning you,' and 'On their hands they will bear you up, lest you strike your foot against a stone.'" Jesus said to him, "Again it is written, 'You shall not put the Lord your God to the test.'" Again, the devil took him to a very high mountain and showed him all the kingdoms of the world and their glory. And he said to him, "All these I will give you, if you will fall down and worship me." Then Jesus said to him, "Be gone, Satan! For it is written,

"'You shall worship the Lord your God and him only shall you serve.'" Then the devil left him, and behold, angels came and were ministering to him." (Matthew 4:1-11)

Satan tempted Jesus in all three of the ways he tempts us. John tells us in his first epistle (I John 2:16) what these three areas are:

(1) the lust of the flesh,
(2) the pride of life, and
(3) the lust of the eyes.

First, Satan tempted Jesus with the lust of the flesh. Jesus had not eaten for forty days and nights and He was hungry. Jesus could have easily turned those stones into bread, but He did not give into His flesh. Instead, He answered Satan by quoting Deuteronomy 8:3. Jesus said, "*No! For the Scriptures tell us, that bread alone won't feed men's souls: obedience to every Word of God is what he needs.*"

Second, Satan tempted Jesus with the pride of life. He was appealing to the attitude that says, "If you are so great, prove it! If you are the Son of God, prove it! If you are who you claim to be, prove it! God will send His angels to protect you." Satan knows the Scriptures. Human pride would have responded to Satan's challenge. We would have said, "Okay, I'll prove it to you!" Jesus answered Satan by quoting Deuteronomy 6:16. "*It also says not to put the Lord your God to a foolish test.*"

Third, Satan tempted Jesus with the lust of the eyes. Satan took Jesus to the top of the highest mountain. From there, they could see all the wealth and splendor of all the Kingdoms of the World. Satan has dominion over the earth since the fall of man through Adam's sin. So he had every right to claim to own the Kingdoms of the World. Jesus did not challenge his right to offer the wealth of the world to Him. Satan said, "*I'll give it all to you, if you only kneel and worship me.*" Jesus responded with, "*Get out of here Satan.*" And then He quoted Deuteronomy 6:13. "*Worship only the Lord God. Obey only Him.*" Then Satan went away. We have been told to resist the devil and He will flee from us. Here Jesus has given us an example of how to do this. Jesus used the Word of God as a sword to drive Satan away. We too can use the Sword of the Spirit, the Word of God, to drive Satan away and out of our lives - if we know the Word and how to use it.

I use the Word of God to drive Satan out of my life

DAILY MEDITATION ON THE WORD BRINGS SUCCESS

Our problem is that we think that just a casual reading of the Word is all we need. We are told, however, to study the Word (II Timothy 2:15). He also said to meditate on and do what the Word says. When Joshua took over leadership of Israel from Moses, God told Joshua, *"This Book of the Law shall not depart from your mouth, but you shall meditate on it day and night, so that you may be careful to do according to all that is written in it. For then you will make your way prosperous, and then you will have good success."* (Joshua 1:8)

We cannot hope to know God's Word by just occasionally leafing through it. The Word of God is our spiritual food and we must eat from it daily in order to rely on it for guidance. If it is to be our instrument panel to fly by, we had better know and understand God's Word very well. We cannot do this piecemeal. We must go to the Bread of Life daily. This is well illustrated by the way God provided food for the children of Israel in the wilderness.

> *"And the LORD said to Moses, "I have heard the grumbling of the people of Israel. Say to them, 'At twilight you shall eat meat, and in the morning you shall be filled with bread. Then you shall know that I am the LORD your God.'"*

> *"In the evening, quail came up and covered the camp, and in the morning dew lay around the camp. And when the dew had gone up, there was on the face of the wilderness a fine, flake-like thing, fine as frost on the ground. When the people of Israel saw it, they said to one another, "What is it?"*

> *For they did not know what it was. And Moses said to them, "It is the bread that the* L*ORD has given you to eat."*
>
> *"This is what the* L*ORD has commanded: 'Gather of it, each one of you, as much as he can eat. You shall each take an omer according to the number of the persons that each of you has in his tent.'" And the people of Israel did so. They gathered some more, some less. But when they measured it with an omer, whoever gathered much had nothing left over, and whoever gathered little had no lack. Each of them gathered as much as he could eat. And Moses said to them, "Let no one leave any of it over till the morning."" "But they did not listen to Moses. Some left part of it till the morning, and it bred worms and stank. And Moses was angry with them. Morning by morning they gathered it, each as much as he could eat; but when the sun grew hot, it melted".* (Exodus 16:11-21)

I go to God's Word every day for the spiritual food I need for that day

When Jesus was teaching the disciples to pray, He said, "*Give us this day our daily bread.*" (Matthew 6:11) Jesus also said, *"Therefore do not be anxious about tomorrow, for tomorrow will be anxious for itself. Sufficient for the day is its own trouble."* (Matthew 6:34) God gave us the principle that He provides for us on a day-to-day basis, not week-to-week, or month-to-month. We need to go to Him each day for the spiritual food for the day. In order to be spiritually strong, we must receive sustenance from His Word daily.

To put on this sixth piece of armor means reading, studying and obeying God's Word every day. This allows it to determine the thoughts and intents of our heart. We must hide God's Word in our heart so that we might not sin against Him. Satan cannot stand against the Word of God.

Chapter Eleven

A LIFE OF HIS WORD

Questions for home study and group discussion

What does the Word of God do for us?
Hebrews 4:12

How can we keep from sin?
Psalm 119:9, 11

In what three ways are we tempted?
I John 2:16

How did Jesus handle temptation?
Matthew 4:1-11

How are we to succeed and prosper?
Joshua 1:8

Notes from My Mentor's Personal Experiences

Scripture Memory Session Eleven

"For the word of God is living and active, sharper than any two-edged sword, piercing to the division of soul and of spirit, of joints and of marrow, and discerning the thoughts and intentions of the heart." (Hebrews 4:12)

CHAPTER TWELVE

A LIFE OF PRAYER

"Ask, and it will be given to you; seek, and you will find; knock, and it will be opened to you. For everyone who asks receives, and the one who seeks finds, and to the one who knocks it will be opened." (Matthew 7:7-8)

Prayer is our means of transmission keeping us in direct communication with our commander. *"Praying at all times in the Spirit, with all prayer and supplication. To that end keep alert with all perseverance, making supplication for all the saints,"* (Ephesians 6:18)

> "Paul admonishes us to put on the whole armor of God in order to stand against the forces of hell. It is clear that our warfare is not against physical forces, but against invisible powers, which have clearly defined levels of authority in a real, though invisible, sphere of activity. Paul, however, not only warns us of a clearly defined structure in the invisi-

> ble realm, he instructs us to take up the whole armor of God in order to maintain a "battle stance" against this unseen satanic structure.
>
> This armor is not just a passive protection in facing the enemy; it is to be used offensively against these satanic forces. Note Paul's final directive that we are to be "praying always with all prayer and supplication in the Spirit." Thus, prayer is not so much a weapon, or even a part of the armor, as it is the means by which we engage in the battle itself and the purpose for which we are armed. To put on the armor of God is to prepare for battle. Prayer is the battle itself, with God's Word being our chief weapon employed against Satan during our struggle." (Spirit Filled Life Bible, page 1797, Kingdom Dynamics).

A soldier on the battlefield communicates his position to the command post. The commander provides heavy artillery where needed to stop the enemy's attacks. We are not in this battle alone. God stands ready to send in the big guns as we request them. He gives us the overall picture of the battle. He shares His intelligence about the enemy's battle plan. He tells us what to do to effectively defeat the enemy on every front. "Pray always." We must constantly keep our radio tuned into our commander's frequency. We must hear from God through His Word, and speak to Him

I hear from God through His Word and speak to Him through my prayers

through prayer. Prayer is impossible without faith. Faith is God's frequency. In order to put our faith in God to guide us through life's circumstances, we need to know what prayer is. We need to know how we are to go about praying so that God hears and answers our prayers.

WHAT IS PRAYER?

What is prayer? Prayer is asking God to meet us at our point of need and believing that when we ask He answers.

> *"Ask, and it will be given to you; seek, and you will find; knock, and it will be opened to you. For everyone who asks receives, and the one who seeks finds, and to the one who knocks it will be opened."* (Matthew 7:7-8)

Prayer is asking and receiving; it is talking to God. It is making our requests known unto Him in faith. Even though the above Scripture seems so simple on the surface that we may fail to recognize its immensity. Our Lord instructs the believer to ask, seek, and knock because these three words cover all the important aspects of prayer.

1. Prayer is asking and receiving

When you know the will of God regarding a need, whether it is material or spiritual, you can ask and receive. This is praying according to the revealed will of God.

> *"And this is the confidence that we have toward him, that if we ask anything according to his will he hears us. And if we know that he hears us in whatever we ask, we*

> *know that we have the requests that we have asked of him."* (I John 5:14-15)

2. Prayer is seeking and finding

When you do not know the will of God regarding a need, whether it is material or spiritual, then you are to seek His will in prayer concerning this need until you find it. This is prayer for knowledge of the unrevealed will of God in a specific need. *"Then you will call upon me and come and pray to me, and I will hear you. You will seek me and find me, when you seek me with all your heart."* (Jeremiah 29:12-13) *"If then you have been raised with Christ, seek the things that are above, where Christ is, seated at the right hand of God."* (Colossians 3:1)

God wants to answer my prayers and I believe He will answer them

3. Prayer is knocking and opening

When you know the will of God and yet you find a closed door, you are to knock and keep knocking until God opens the door. This is tenacious prayer, prayer for mountain moving faith. Knocking prayer perseveres until the impossible becomes the possible. This is miracle-working prayer.

> *"And he said to them, "Which of you who has a friend will go to him at midnight and say to him, 'Friend, lend me three loaves, for a friend of mine has arrived on a journey, and I have nothing to set before him'; and he will answer from within, 'Do not bother me; the door is now shut, and my*

children are with me in bed. I cannot get up and give you anything'? I tell you, though he will not get up and give him anything because he is his friend, yet because of his impudence he will rise and give him whatever he needs." (Luke 11:5-8)

All things are possible when I ask, seek, and knock

All things are possible when we ask, seek, and knock. One day Jesus told His disciples a story to illustrate their need for constant prayer and to show them that they must persist in pray until the answer comes.

"He said, "In a certain city there was a judge who neither feared God nor respected man. And there was a widow in that city who kept coming to him and saying, 'Give me justice against my adversary.' For a while he refused, but afterward he said to himself, 'Though I neither fear God nor respect man, yet because this widow keeps bothering me, I will give her justice, so that she will not beat me down by her continual coming.'" And the Lord said, "Hear what the unrighteous judge says. And will not God give justice to his elect, who cry to him day and night? Will he delay long over them? I tell you, he will give justice to them speedily. Nevertheless, when the Son of Man comes, will he find faith on earth?" (Luke 18:2-8)

WHY PRAY? TEN REASONS TO PRAY

1. We need to pray
   "*Watch and pray that you may not enter into temptation. The spirit indeed is willing, but the flesh is weak.*" (Matthew 26:41)

2. We are to pray because it is one way to get things from God
   "*You desire and do not have, so you murder. You covet and cannot obtain, so you fight and quarrel. You do not have, because you do not ask.*" (James 4:2)

3. Prayer brings joy to the believer
   "*In that day you will ask nothing of me. Truly, truly, I say to you, whatever you ask of the Father in my name, he will give it to you. Until now you have asked nothing in my name. Ask, and you will receive, that your joy may be full.*" (John 16:23-24)

4. Prayer will deliver us out of our troubles
   "*I sought the LORD, and he answered me, and delivered me from all my fears. … This poor man cried, and the LORD heard him and saved him out of all his troubles. … When the righteous cry for help, the LORD hears and delivers them out of all their troubles.*" (Psalm 34:4, 6, 17)

5. Prayer can unlock the treasure of God's wisdom.
   "*If any of you lacks wisdom, let him ask God, who gives generously to all without reproach, and it will be given him.*" (James 1:5)

6. Prayer is a channel of power.
   "*Call to me and I will answer you, and will tell you great and hidden things that you have not known.*" (Jeremiah 33:3)

7. It is sin not to pray.
   Moreover, as for me, far be it from me that I should sin against the L*ORD* *by ceasing to pray for you, and I will instruct you in the good and the right way.*" (I Samuel 12:23)

8. Sinners can be saved when they pray in faith.
   "*Everyone who calls on the name of the Lord will be saved.*" (Romans 10:13)

9. We are to follow Jesus' example.
   Now if Jesus, the Son of God, needed to pray, how much more then are we in need of prayer. "*Pray without ceasing.*" (I Thessalonians 5:17)

10. Pray expectantly to receive the answer we want.
    "*Truly, I say to you, whoever says to this mountain, 'Be taken up and thrown into the sea,' and does not doubt in his heart, but believes that what he says will come to pass, it will be done for him. Therefore, I tell you, whatever you ask in prayer, believe*

that you have received it, and it will be yours." (Mark 11: 23-24)

(While writing this book in prison, the only study Bible I had was the Open Bible. Therefore, most of the outline of the above section on "What is Prayer?" and "Why Pray?" is an adaptation of the reference notes on the bottom of pages 893 and 973. Used by permission)

GOD DESIRES OUR FELLOWSHIP IN PRAYER

God wants to answer our prayers. But we must believe that He will answer. Why pray if you don't believe God will answer? God desires our fellowship in prayer. God is love, and He loves us with an eternal and unconditional love. Because he loves us so much, He longs for our fellowship. We were created for the purpose of fellowship with God; that we might glorify Him by freely giving our love and devotion to Him.

I glorify God by freely giving my love and devotion to Him

Because of our right-standing with God, through Christ, we are told that we are to go boldly into God's very presence. I have often imagined what it would be like to be in the presence of God. Since we have access to the "Holy of Holies," we can go right into God's throne room.

I can imagine the brilliance of God radiating from His throne. The Holy Spirit is there as a crystal stream flowing from the throne. Jesus is sitting at the right side of God the Father. The Accuser of the Brethren, Satan, is popping in and out, to accuse the saints before God. Then there I am, sitting in the middle of it all, talking to my Heavenly Father.

As I enter the throne room, everybody's attention is on me. I bow before God in humble adoration, realizing that I am in the presence of God, who with His very words spoke all that there is into existence. He looks at me lovingly and tells me to be seated. All I can do is just praise God and express my love and joy at being a member of His family. I start to confess some sin when The Accuser appears, from what seemed like nowhere. He starts reeling off a whole list of sins from my past. But Jesus stands up and says, "Father, all of Roy's sins have been covered by my blood at Calvary. Because of Roy's faith in my death, burial, and resurrection, there is nothing left that Roy can be accused of; it is all forgiven." Satan flees the throne room as quickly as he arrived.

I constantly thank God because I realize how much He loves me

I begin to thank God. I realize how much God loves me. It is also apparent that He loves the time we had to share together. He seems disappointed that I don't come more often and stay longer. I am so thankful that my life is totally under the control of a Father who loves me so much. I know He wants the best for me.

Then I share my needs. There is no doubt that my Father wants more for me than I want for myself, and that He knows what I really need. Everything I ask for was done before I even ask. Of course, I do my best to ask according to what I know God's Word promises that I can have in the name of Jesus. I mention several needs of my family and friends. My Heavenly Father assures me that He will supply all their needs according to His riches in glory by Christ Jesus.

I spend as much time with my Father as possible, but finally I have to get ready for work. My face beaming, my heart filled with joy, I say to Him, "Continue to walk with me throughout the day, Father!"

Even though I am just imagining the above, it's very much the way I understand the Scriptures as they apply to prayer, our fellowship with God in prayer, our requests according to His will, and His answering our prayers.

A PERSONAL EXPERIENCE

God's love for me became especially real when I was separated from my wife, Sarah. I had been arrested and confined to jail. I had no way of contacting her to tell her how very much I loved her. I longed to communicate with her and tell her that no matter what happened, my love would always be there for her.

After being booked, I was allowed to use the telephone. It was so good to hear her voice and to reassure her of my love, as well as to hear her tell me that her love would always be there for me no matter what. I believe God longs for us to come to Him so that He can reassure us of His love and hear us express our love to Him.

Several days passed and I ached inside with my missing of Sarah. I longed to see her. I prayed that God would see my need and bring Sarah to me. I knew that she must be hurting and I wanted to know that she was all right. Then came the day I was called by the deputy and was told that I had a visitor. I was sent to a room where there was a long row of seats with windows and a telephone at each. I went to my assigned seat and anxiously waited. Soon she appeared. As I gazed through the window to the other side, there was my beautiful wife. She picked up the phone and we began to talk. How I longed for her. But we could not touch or hold each other.

The window separated us. I wanted so much to have a deeper and closer fellowship, but this wasn't to be. This form of visiting went on for over six months. She visited me faithfully at least once or twice a week, and the fifteen to twenty minutes we were allowed was very precious to me. How I longed to hold her and share our love more intimately. It must be something like the way God longs to have a deeper relationship with each of us when we have something keeping us from an open intimate relationship with Him.

I received a four-year sentence and was sent to the California State Prison, uncertain of what to expect. Upon arriving, I was shattered to learn that I would not have access to a telephone. Sarah seemed far away and my missing her grew with each day. Then one day, I heard my name paged over the prison address system, directing me to report to the visiting room. As I entered, my heart swelled, my eyes began to mist, for there was my Sarah, standing there waiting for me. No phones and no windows to separate us. I took her in my arms and we held one another, neither one wanted to let go. How good she felt! We were able to sit and visit for six hours. We talked, we hugged, and we enjoyed every minute of our time together. After that first visit, Sarah came to see me at least once a week. Each one was as special and meaningful as the first. Our hearts touched as we were once again together, and our love for one another grew even stronger. I looked forward to each and every one of those visits with all my heart.

If God loves me as much as I love Sarah, He must long for the time we spend together. Of course, God is love! Therefore, He loves me even more than I love Sarah.

A special time came. I was informed that I was approved for a family visit. Sarah and I could spend forty-eight hours alone together in a furnished trailer provided by the prison. We had been apart for eleven months and now we were able to share our love for one another in the most intimate way. We had a wonderful time, but the hands on the clock passed too quickly. We enjoyed each other ever so much and each minute together became more precious than the last. We discovered newness in our love, and that our love had grown stronger than it was before our separation. From that time on, we looked forward to and counted the months between each family visit.

I believe that God also longs for the intimacy of our fellowship with Him. When we pray in the Spirit, it is the most personal fellowship we can have with Him. If God enjoys this deep fellowship with His children as much as Sarah and I enjoyed our sweet love and fellowship, then He must be miserable when we don't come to Him and spend that special time in His presence, praying in the Spirit.

God loves me even more than I love my wife/ husband

HOW SHOULD WE PRAY?

An acrostic that I learned as a young believer and still use in prayer is A.C.T.S. It may help you to have a format by which to enter into prayer.

A - IS FOR ATTITUDE

When we pray, our attitude is the most important element. We need to have an attitude of adoration, worship, humility, and expectation. The Psalms are probably the best place to learn how to worship and adore God. Following are a few verses from Psalm 95:

> *"For the LORD is a great God, and a great King above all gods. In his hand are the depths of the earth; the heights of the mountains are his also. The sea is his, for he made it, and his hands formed the dry land. Oh come, let us worship and bow down; let us*

> *kneel before the LORD, our Maker! He is our God, and we are the people of his pasture, and the sheep of his hand."* (Psalm 95:3-7)

C - IS FOR CONFESSION

Confession means to acknowledge that we agree with God that what we have done is sin. *"For I am ready to fall, and my pain is ever before me. I confess my iniquity; I am sorry for my sin."* (Psalm 38:17-18) *"If we say we have no sin, we deceive ourselves, and the truth is not in us. If we confess our sins, he is faithful and just to forgive us our sins and to cleanse us from all unrighteousness. If we say we have not sinned, we make him a liar, and his word is not in us."* (I John 1:8-10)

T - IS FOR THANKSGIVING

When we realize what God has done for us, we can't help but be thankful. He has restored us to right-standing with Himself through Christ Jesus. After we have confessed our sin to Him, there is nothing between us. We are as righteous as Jesus in the sight of God our Heavenly Father. We have been justified, which means in God's eyes that we are just as if we had never sinned. We can't help but praise the Lord for all that he has freely done, because He loves us so much. There are many verses of Scripture that remind us to thank and praise the Lord.

> *"And now we thank you, our God, and praise your glorious name."* (I Chronicles 29:13) *"To you, O God of my fathers, I give thanks and praise, for you have given me wisdom and might, and have now made known to me what we asked of you, for you have made known to us the king's matter."*

> (Daniel 2:23) *"But I with the voice of thanksgiving will sacrifice to you; what I have vowed I will pay. Salvation belongs to the LORD!"* (Jonah 2:9) *"Let us come into his presence with thanksgiving; let us make a joyful noise to him with songs of praise!* (Psalm 95:2) *"rooted and built up in him and established in the faith, just as you were taught, abounding in thanksgiving."* (Colossians 2:7)

S - IS FOR SUPPLICATION

Supplication is to pray for your needs as well as the needs of others. Paul tells us about prayer. He says, *"praying at all times in the Spirit, with all prayer and supplication. To that end keep alert with all perseverance, making supplication for all the saints,"* (Ephesians 6:18)

> *"Likewise the Spirit helps us in our weakness. For we do not know what to pray for as we ought, but the Spirit himself intercedes for us with groaning's too deep for words. And he who searches hearts knows what is the mind of the Spirit, because the Spirit intercedes for the saints according to the will of God."* (Romans 8:26-27)

We must pray daily in order to keep the lines of communication open. Our Heavenly Father loves to share this special time with us. Don't let Satan convince you that because of your sins, you are not worthy to pray. You pray because

> *My full armor is in place so that I can battle effectively*

you're not worthy. If we were worthy in and of ourselves, Jesus Christ would not have had to die to bring us into right-standing with God. Satan wants you to dwell on your sin so that you will always feel that you cannot come into the presence of God. He doesn't want you to claim the promises that God gives in His Word.

God's love for you is so strong that there is no sin great enough that would keep God from welcoming you with open arms when you come to Him. During your fellowship with God the Father, God the Holy Spirit will help you to see where you need to agree with God regarding areas of sin that need to be dealt with. When you acknowledge that a certain area of your life is sin, it is forgiven immediately. God's forgiveness is total and instantaneous.

Trust God's love. Come to Him each day, no matter what you've done or think you've done. If nothing else, just adore Him. Worship His holiness. God loves you with an eternal, unconditional love. He does not sit in Heaven waiting to zap you just because you've done something wrong. We often relate the way our parents treated us to the way we expect God to treat us. Some of us had parents who attacked us violently when we did something wrong. So our anticipation is that God will do the same thing to us. God does not do that. He wants to restore you back into perfect fellowship with Himself.

WE MUST PRAY EVERY DAY

"Therefore do not be anxious about tomorrow, for tomorrow will be anxious for itself. Sufficient for the day is its own trouble." (Matthew 6:34) In other words, live one day at a time. The great thing about living one day at a time is that you can't relive the past. It is gone and finished. So let it go! Confess it and forget it! God did. You can't live tomorrow, so don't worry about tomorrow. You can only live today. So live it to God's glory. Don't let your past or your future rob you of the wonderful relationship you have with your Heavenly Father today. Pray today. Now!

Each piece of armor is necessary in order to have victory over the enemy and his huge army of spiritual emissaries. Even though prayer is considered the battlefield, the full armor must be in place in order for us to do battle effectively. Without the knowledge of God's Word, without knowing you are saved for all eternity, without absolute faith in God's provision, without preparation to share the gospel, without your position of right-standing in God's family, and without truth, our prayer life is weak and powerless to defeat Satan.

Put on the whole armor of God through daily prayer in the name of Jesus. The Holy Spirit will guide you when you don't know what to pray for or how to pray. We need to know how to put on the full armor of God. Others will emulate us as they see how effectively we fight the battle against Satan and his army. They will watch to see if we tell the truth, reflect righteousness as our position in Christ, share the gospel, demonstrate faith in God's provision during trying circumstances, show our trust in Jesus Christ for our eternal destiny, defeat Satan with the Word of God, and win the real battle against the unseen forces while praying always in the Spirit's power.

Chapter Twelve

A LIFE OF PRAYER

Questions for home study and group discussion

What are the three elements making up the full spectrum of prayer?
Matthew 7:7-8

When we know God's will about a need, but do not get an answer to our prayers, what should we do? Luke 11:5-8, 18:1-8

Give at least four reasons why we should pray. (The answer is found in this chapter.)

What is the acrostic that reminds us of what to do when we pray? Explain each word in the acrostic. (The answer is found in this chapter.)

Why should we spend time every day in prayer?
Matthew 6:34

Notes from My Mentor's Personal Experiences

Scripture Memory Chapter Twelve

"Ask, and it will be given to you; seek, and you will find; knock, and it will be opened to you. For everyone who asks receives, and the one who seeks finds, and to the one who knocks it will be opened." (Matthew 7:7-8)

FOUR SPIRITUAL CHARACTERISTICS OF A GODLY LIFE

SPIRITUAL CHARACTERISTIC ONE

BEING A BELIEVER

I know Jesus Christ as my personal Lord and Savior

SPIRITUAL CHARACTERISTIC TWO

BEING EMPOWERED

I am controlled and empowered by the Holy Spirit

SPIRITUAL CHARACTERISTIC THREE

BEING VICTORIOUS

I have Christ's authority over all of the enemy's power

SPIRITUAL CHARACTERISTIC FOUR

BEING A WARRIOR

I put on all of God's armor in order to defeat Satan

ABOUT THE AUTHOR

Dr. Roy Comstock, author of Mentoring His Way, Disciple Twelve, is a man who has had many unique life experiences. In his early childhood days, he was forced to adapt to living in fourteen different foster homes. As an ambitious businessman, he saw the rise and fall of his own multi-million-dollar corporation, which led to the humbling adjustment of a life in prison confinement. This was a lesson in what can happen to a Christian who dares to take their eyes off Jesus for a time.

This book has not been written by a perfect man or by one whose life has always been a model for others to follow. Roy's life has not always been easy. He, like all true Christians, has been and is a work of God "in process." We may call this Roy Comstock's "Prison Epistle," since much of this material was written while he was serving a prison term.

Roy experienced major failure to his marriage, his business, and his personal life because of his misguided focus on self rather than on Christ. But Roy repented and turned to Christ in a deeper way than ever before. He cried out to the Lord concerning his own life, and the Lord responded not only to his needs, but also taught him insights that can be of great help to anyone who desires to truly follow Jesus Christ. It was during his time in prison that the Lord revealed many of the principles that Roy calls the "Twelve Characteristics of a Godly Life."

Roy and his wife Sarah, live in Valencia, California.

Hope - Confident expectancy
not wishful
thinking firm
assurance about
[illegible]

CPSIA information can be obtained
at www.ICGtesting.com
Printed in the USA
FFOW03n1348180218
45057375-45446FF

9 781635 752892